Practicing Mindfulness

Practicing Mindfulness

Finding Calm and Focus in Your Everyday Life

Jerry Braza

Foreword by
Thich Nhat Hanh

TUTTLE Publishing

Tokyo | Rutland, Vermont | Singapore

"Books to Span the East and West"

Tuttle Publishing was founded in 1832 in the small New England town of Rutland, Vermont [USA]. Our core values remain as strong today as they were then—to publish best-in-class books which bring people together one page at a time. In 1948, we established a publishing outpost in Japan—and Tuttle is now a leader in publishing English-language books about the arts, languages and cultures of Asia. The world has become a much smaller place today and Asia's economic and cultural influence has grown. Yet the need for meaningful dialogue and information about this diverse region has never been greater. Over the past seven decades, Tuttle has published thousands of books on subjects ranging from martial arts and paper crafts to language learning and literature—and our talented authors, illustrators, designers and photographers have won many prestigious awards. We welcome you to explore the wealth of information available on Asia at **www.tuttlepublishing.com.**

Published by Tuttle Publishing, an imprint of Periplus Editions (HK) Ltd.

www.tuttlepublishing.com

ISBN 978-0-8048-5260-9

Distributed by

North America, Latin America & Europe
Tuttle Publishing
364 Innovation Drive, North Clarendon,
VT 05759-9436 U.S.A.
Tel: (802) 773-8930
Fax: (802) 773-6993
info@tuttlepublishing.com
www.tuttlepublishing.com

Japan
Tuttle Publishing
Yaekari Building,
3rd Floor, 5-4-12 Osaki, Shinagawa-ku,
Tokyo 141 0032
Tel: (81) 3 5437-0171
Fax: (81) 3 5437-0755
sales@tuttle.co.jp; www.tuttle.co.jp

Asia Pacific
Berkeley Books Pte. Ltd.
3 Kallang Sector #04-01/02,
Singapore 349278
Tel: (65) 6741 2178
Fax: (65) 6741 2179
inquiries@periplus.com.sg
www.tuttlepublishing.com

First edition
26 25 24 5 4 3

Printed in China 2311CM

Contents

Foreword

by Thich Nhat Hanh

Mindfulness is the basis for transforming ourselves and creating a more harmonious family and society. It is the miracle that allows us to become fully alive in each moment. The deepest fruit of mindfulness practice is the realization that peace and joy are available, within us and around us, right here and now. This is something we can taste, and we can offer it to everyone we meet and everyone we love.

In *Practicing Mindfulness*, Dr. Jerry Braza suggests many simple exercises in which to apply the practice of mindfulness to our daily lives. I congratulate him for offering such thoughtful, creative and clear explanations of the practical benefits of practicing mindfulness. This is a very useful guide for living mindfully. I hope you will return to it again and again and practice wholeheartedly the exercises Dr. Braza offers.

Acknowledgments

I am profoundly grateful to the many people who have walked with me and offered deeper understanding of the practice of mindfulness.

First, I bow to Zen Master Thich Nhat Hanh, who has been my teacher for more than 30 years. He ordained me as a dharma teacher 20 years ago, and offered an ongoing connection with him and his worldwide lineage of teachers and practitioners. That community provided the inspiration for this book.

My wife, Kathleen, has offered continual support and provides a mirror for the practice of mindfulness. She listens to my joys and struggles and has always been there to nurture me and encourage me to seek opportunities for practice. Kathleen has been an astute editor, reviewing and improving each chapter as it emerged. Most important, her loving presence in my life has been an example of kindness and compassion—the heart of this book.

My son, Mark Braza, and daughter, Andrea Godfrey, offered me firsthand experiences in practicing mindfulness; they knew me as a young dad and provided feedback as to how my practice was going. I hope they witnessed a gradual awakening. Mark is an environmental health scientist at the General Accountability Office in Washington, D.C. Andrea lives in Geneva, Switzerland, where she works at the World Health Organization. They understand what it means to make a difference in the lives of others.

The current edition of this book was supported by my

spiritual friend and editor, Nadene LeCheminant. Her understanding of the practice of mindfulness is a reflection of her being, and with her editing acumen, she gently critiqued and helped frame my words to make them more beautiful.

Tuttle Publishing has offered invaluable support. During our 25-year relationship, their belief in my work and writing has been a mainstay. This rewrite is the third book they have supported, including *The Seeds of Love*. I am indebted to editor Doug Sanders, who has been a critical guide in mindfully reviewing and taking this project through the publication process.

My philosophy was deepened and supported by two deceased monks—Phap De (Adrian Stier), a former Catholic priest who became a Buddhist monk, and Brother Mark Filut, a Catholic monk who resided at the local Trappist Abbey. They helped understand that a connection with God, the divine and ultimate is possible!

Special gratitude goes to those inspirational teachers whose writings and teachings resonate with me in an almost mystical way. They include Jon Kabat-Zinn, Joan Halifax, Tara Brach, Jack Kornfield, John O'Donohue, Rick Hanson, The Dalai Lama, Bessel Van der Kolk, Richard Rohr, Ram Dass, Jack Kornfield, Stephen Levine, Elisabeth Kubler-Ross and Carl Rogers. Their guidance has inspired me, and I humbly hope my writings reflect their wisdom.

Anam Cara Friends on the path include Werner Brandt, Bob Brevoort, Charles Busch, Geoff Colvin, Jack Curtis, Dave Disorbio, Gary Gach, Ann Martin, Nisi Segor, Joe Spader, Tom Stella and John Wadsworth. These dear friends have been open to shining a light on my reflections and journey.

To you, the readers—thank you for picking up this book! I trust it will support you in your journey to find happiness in each moment.

Introduction

Often, if we pay attention, when we come to a challenging fork in the road of life, a book falls from a shelf, or a friend shares a story, or we find the perfect quote to highlight our journey ahead and, magically, a path appears or a new door opens.

In the mid-1980s, as a college professor and divorced dad with two children, I found myself preoccupied with stress-related chest pains. I was just getting by and the road ahead did not seem to offer healing answers. It was at that time I attended a conference in which the keynote speaker was Dr. Elisabeth Kübler-Ross, who is credited for popularizing the "five stages of grief." She said, "At the end of life, we do not remember things—our jobs, our money. What we remember are moments, especially moments with loved ones."

Soon after, in a training workshop with well-known humanistic psychologist Carl Rogers, I witnessed firsthand the powerful modeling of emotional presence and wondered: How does one learn and practice such a strong awareness of the present moment? I began to study the work of various meditation teachers such as Ram Dass, Jack Kornfield and Stephen Levine. From their teachings, the word "mindfulness" surfaced, and "be here now" became my mantra.

Several years later a friend gifted me with a book titled *The Miracle of Mindfulness* and I discovered that mindfulness was more than a concept—it was a practice! With this gift, and aware that I learn best through experience and teaching, I created a summer workshop on mindfulness at the University of Utah. Mindfulness soon became the core of my classes and consulting, and I made the decision to go beyond knowing to being, to try to actually live a mindful life.

In 1991 I had my first significant encounter with Buddhist Master Thich Nhat Hanh at a retreat at the Omega Institute in New York. Sitting in the dharma hall with hundreds of others, I observed him mindfully walk across a field toward the meditation hall and I knew in that moment that he would be my teacher. Inspired by this humble Vietnamese monk, I wrote a book, *Moment by Moment: The Art and Practice of Mindfulness*. Thay was kind enough to write the foreword, as it was one of the first books enunciating the practice of mindfulness in his tradition.

A lot has happened in the field of mindfulness since this book was first published in 1997. Now mindfulness is not only a household word; it has become one of the most popular research topics. Many people have benefitted by incorporating this practice into their lives. In some sense, the late 1990s, when the first edition of this book came out, seemed to be a simpler time. Today we are exposed to more stressors than ever, including the frantic pace of our lifestyles and the 24/7 lure of media, with its ever-present bad news cycle. Mindfulness is more relevant than ever.

The original edition of *Moment by Moment* was published in six languages. Readers have shared examples of how the book has been used as a beginning point for the practice of mindfulness, and how these simple ideas ignited an awareness that life could be more abundant. The original copy has been used by hundreds of people—from university students to health care workers to oil workers in Prudhoe Bay, Alaska. A psychiatrist in Geneva, Switzerland, uses the French edition of this book for his patients.

One of my favorite stories of how the original book changed someone's life comes from Brett Moran, a man from the United Kingdom who has become an author, motivational speaker and retreat leader. His life was very different as a young man; he was addicted to crack cocaine, selling drugs on the streets, and suicidal. He ended up in prison, where he came across *Moment by Moment* in the prison library. During his time behind bars, he read the book cover to cover at least ten times and began to spend his days practicing the simple mindfulness techniques. He said, "The more I read, the calmer I started to feel." Seventeen years later, Moran lives in Thailand, where he leads yoga and meditation retreats. He says, "*Moment by Moment* will help you understand the nature of your mind and set you on a path of healing and transformation. If you are ready to let go of who you think you are and challenge your old programmed thoughts, you'll discover your deeper essence. *Moment by Moment* was a catalyst for igniting my personal transformation all those years ago."

The practice of mindfulness still works. In this twenty-fifth anniversary edition, you are about to discover and hopefully begin to experience one of the oldest and most profound strategies for enhancing health, relationships, productivity and happiness. Mindfulness is the practice of becoming fully aware of each moment and one's experience in that moment. Rooted in ancient traditions, this practice reminds us of how precious life is.

A few years ago, a friend who practiced with our meditation group and was suffering from stage IV cancer, found that mindfulness was the best medicine. It helped him to enjoy life while going through a myriad of tests, multiple surgeries and chemotherapy. He lived seven years with his diagnosis and often commented on how this was the first time in his 80-plus years that he was truly in touch with the present moment. The message etched on his niche at the mausoleum where he now rests is borrowed from a song by French singer Edith Piaf: *Non, je ne regrette rien*. "I have no regrets." That message speaks to me each day.

As you begin this journey, you might explore in your own life how you may have changed over the years, from a more natural state of *being* to an overriding state of *doing*? The seeds of mindfulness are sometimes formed early in life, but I was the type of individual who lived, not for *this* moment, but for the next moment. I would skip pages when reading bedtime stories to my children. On family vacations, my primary focus was to get there rather than to enjoy the journey. Through meditation (which simply means "to attend to") I began to transform my way of looking at life. My experience has been that sometimes people enjoy life less because they miss it along the way. While we are making plans and looking ahead and regretting the past, we miss out on life in the here and now.

When this book was first written, mindfulness was just beginning to be viewed as a viable practice that nourishes overall well-being and helps individuals stay anchored while coping with the stressors in life. Today, mindfulness has become fully accepted as a support to patients and professionals in the field of mental and physical health. Extensive research supports its benefits, and programs like the one developed by Jon Kabat-Zinn, Mindfulness-Based Stress Reduction (MBSR), are being used to ameliorate numerous health problems. After a critical review of the literature in the field of health and psychology, I discovered virtually hundreds of different strategies for achieving well-being and happiness. However, it became clear to me that the simple practice of mindfulness is a good place to start.

My goal is to help you recall what you already know and reawaken your spirit to the beauty and joy that exists in every moment. Practicing mindfulness can become a tool that helps you learn how to regain that natural state of joy and discovery so recognizable in young children, that state of appreciation for each moment as it is experienced for the first time. Learning to become more mindful provides an alternative to living mindlessly or mechanically.

The reader is encouraged to use this book as a companion and guide to abundant living. Take time to pause, reflect and open this book to any suggestion that seems relevant to you. Use the book and the practices as part of your daily meditation routine. Learning to be is as important as learning to do—this book encourages us to practice, and with time the words become alive.

Right now, pause and appreciate your breath and aliveness … Through this simple awareness of your breath and the present moment, you have already begun a process that could potentially become a regular practice, even change your life. In this moment, there is health, wholeness and the potential for joy and peace.

Questions to Ponder

As we begin this journey, I invite you to reflect upon the following questions:

- What am I missing right now while I am making other plans?

- What from the past is robbing me of a sense of peace today?

- How often am I with someone yet not really present?

- When challenges arise, am I able to embrace what is happening, and eventually come to the acceptance that "it is what it is"?

- Am I able to transform my own suffering so I don't transmit it to others?

- Am I able to linger longer on the joy that is available in each personal encounter, beautiful sunset or everyday experience?

- In what ways can I become more peaceful in this moment?

- In what moments of my life am I most alive?

- What would my life be like if I lived with this realization: "This is it"?

- The final question, in the form of a quote from Hillel the Elder, born in 110 BCE, is this: *If I am not for myself, then who will be for me? And if I am only for myself, then what am I? And if not now, when?*

Practicing mindfulness will offer insights into these and many more questions that pertain to living your life in a more awakened way. I invite you to consider how the quality of your life can be enhanced by dwelling in the present moment, and to begin a new adventure in mindfulness. Join others who have discovered that this practice is the foundation for a happier life.

PART ONE
An Overview

Do you pay regular visits to yourself? —RUMI

IN PART ONE YOU WILL

- Discover the meaning of mindfulness
- Develop a mindset for cultivating mindfulness
- Learn the importance of mindfulness in your life
- Take the Mindfulness Test

What Is Mindfulness?

If I had to pick one concept that has piqued my curiosity and changed my life in profound ways, it would be "mindfulness." For more than thirty-five years, the idea continues to come alive for me. My early insights were about its potential to enhance well-being; now it has become a way of looking deeply at my relationships.

In my younger years, my spirit and energy were often directed toward the past or future. When I discovered mindfulness, it felt as if it was a panacea for the way I was living my life. At first it was a useful means to manage my stress as a young dad and professor. Later, it became a compass for exploring what was really happening in my daily meditation practice. This helped me to look deeply at my experiences and explore my consciousness and my connections with others. More recently, this practice has taken me on a deeper journey, one that has prompted me to look at my inner shadows, and to embrace the love that emerges from these reflections.

Mindfulness is the natural state of living moment by moment. Observe young children, and you will quickly notice that most of their awareness is focused on the present moment. They are not as concerned with the past or future. I recall an experience from years ago when I was driving my children somewhere. Just as we approached a railroad crossing, the lights began to flash, and the safety gate lowered. My first thought was, "Oh no! We're going to be held up by a train. We'll be late." My thoughts were interrupted by my daughter, who called out excitedly from the back seat, "Daddy, Daddy, we're so lucky! We get to watch the train go by!" Her awareness of the present moment was a wonderful reminder to stop and enjoy the experiences this journey had to offer along the way. Young children can be our teachers of mindfulness as they take delight in the tiny bug crawling on a leaf, the sound of a fish splashing in the stream, and the feel of the sand beneath their feet.

Often, this same awareness is also observable in the elderly or in individuals who are close to death. A former neighbor, terminally ill with cancer, cherished each evening sunset shared with his wife on the front porch, and often expressed a new and profound sense of appreciation for the beauty of his garden and the mountain view. I will always remember sitting with several friends who were receiving chemotherapy; there was both an uncertainty and a fresh awareness regarding the fragility of their lives. Recognition of the preciousness of each moment is more apparent in those who know the end of life is near. As author Joan Borysenko writes, "We are all terminal; the question is not whether we will die but how we are going to live."

Mindfulness is about moments. Psychologist and Nobel Prize winner Daniel Kahneman says that we experience about 20,000 moments each day. In his book, *Thinking Fast and Slow*, he writes that our brains only remember two things about these moments—the emotional peak and the end. Of course, the highs of life are never forgotten, and the conclusions of events are also powerful. I recall many endings that were both challenging and refreshing—a divorce, the completion of a marathon, book projects. Mindfulness is a practice that adds richness to the moments in between, the moments that are easily lost.

Mindset for Mindfulness

Developing mindfulness, like any new behavior, requires a different mindset. Jon Kabat-Zinn, founder of the Stress Reduction Clinic at the University of Massachusetts Medical Center, advocates seven attitudinal foundations of mindfulness: non-judging, patience, a beginner's mind, trust, non-striving, acceptance and letting go. To help you develop a mindset for mindfulness, consider the following:

- **Do you seek instant pain relief and instant pleasure, rather than allowing events to occur at their own pace and time?** Complete openness to each moment requires patience.

- **Do you consider yourself an expert or a beginner?** From Zen philosophy comes the notion of the "beginner's mind," which means that you are learning to experience each moment and activity as if it were for the first time. Children provide excellent models of this concept. In *Zen Mind, Beginner's Mind*, Shunryu Suzuki wrote, "In the beginner's mind there are many possibilities, but in the expert's, there are few."

- **How often do you wait for others to decide before making a personal decision?** Learning to trust yourself rather than looking to others is a key to developing mindfulness. When we observe our body sensations, thoughts and feelings, we become empowered through learning to trust our own intuition.

- **Are you able to be happy in the moment, finding a time to just be each day, without constant striving?** Most of our waking day is spent in *doing*, striving to go somewhere or accomplish something or obtain something. Striving is connected to *doing* and non-striving is connected to *being*. Creating some time each day to just be is difficult, since most of our identity is often based on what we do or accomplish. Developing a proper mindset for mindfulness requires an awareness of being open to anything and everything that is experienced.

- **Do you have a hard time accepting yourself?** In practicing mindfulness, you accept each moment as it comes, and you experience it fully. Acceptance is learned as you observe your body, thoughts, feelings and experiences without judgment. Learning to accept your past, despite the pain, failures and problems, will be difficult unless you learn to accept what is happening in the present.

- **How much of your day do you find yourself ruminating about experiences and people from the past?** Forgiveness means letting go. One of my favorite quotes is, "Hanging on to resentment is allowing someone you despise to live rent-free in your head." If you can simply observe and then let go of these thoughts that arise, it will be easier to let go of the past.

- **Do you find yourself lacking patience and judging yourself and others?** If you tend to be judgmental or lack patience, how can you expect to truly accept others?

There is not one formula that will magically create the state of a mindful lifestyle. Yet, this mindset and these conditions can remind us we are going in the right direction.

Contemplations

Mindfulness is the awareness that arises from paying attention, on purpose, in the present moment —non-judgmentally.

—JON KABAT-ZINN

To live without mindfulness is to live as if we were dead already.

—SHARON SALZBERG

For everything there is a season, and a time for every matter under heaven: A time to be born, and a time to die … a time to kill, and a time to heal … a time to weep, and a time to laugh; a time to mourn, and a time to dance … a time to keep, and a time to cast away …

—ECCLESIASTES

Questions to Ponder

- What does the word mindfulness mean to you?
- Allow yourself time to focus on thoughts as they arise. How many are based on judgment?
- In what ways in your daily life might you use the concepts described in Mindset for Mindfulness?

Why Mindfulness?

Be happy in the moment, that's enough.
Each moment is all we need, not more.

—MOTHER TERESA

Many years ago, on a trip to Southern California with my then five-year-old daughter, we spent time at the typical tourist attractions. We also spent time walking on the beach and writing notes to each other in the sand. Shortly after our return, I asked my daughter what she enjoyed most about the trip. Thinking she would say "Disneyland!" I was surprised and moved by her answer. She said, "The best part was walking down the beach with you, Dad." Whether a person is close to death or living as a child does, what really seems to matter are moments. An awareness of our impermanence can provide motivation to appreciate each moment as if it were our first or last.

Awareness of Impermanence

Moments are fleeting and precious and yet they often don't come to be as meaningful until it is too late.

When friends are challenged by disease and people I love die, this concept comes alive, and as I grow older, these conversations are becoming more relevant and frequent. When I connect with friends, health and death seem to be the first things out of our mouth. These have become like a carillon of bells—a constant wake-up call. We realize that there is less time left to us and feel more of an urgency to savor each experience more fully.

Stress Reduction

The relevance of each moment is often lost when we are occupied with our daily stressors. A high percentage of illness is related to stress—a major concern in health care today. With mindfulness as a guide, we soon become aware that the stressors in our lives are related to our body, thoughts and feelings, and that these stresses are stored in our consciousness. When we recollect joyful childhood experiences, we resurrect memories—happy thoughts and feelings. On the other hand, when we reminisce about old traumas, we fill our present awareness with worry, guilt and fear.

Stress is often the result of being over-committed or engaging in a tendency to rush. Early in my life, I was oftentimes guided by a parental message to hurry. Like many children, I was strongly encouraged to do things quickly. "Hurry and get into the car." "Hurry up or we'll be late." "Hurry with your homework so you can go out and play." Seldom are children or adults praised for moving slowly and deliberately. So, naturally, I learned to rush through my life. As I grew older, I gradually realized that living in the moment may clearly be one of the best-kept secrets for effective stress reduction and wellness.

Increased Productivity

Effectiveness and productivity are enhanced when a person's concentration is improved. When the mind wanders, it is difficult to concentrate. Preoccupation with the past or the future, coupled with "polyphasic thinking" (following many thoughts at one time) results in unfulfilling activities and tasks and a less than meaningful connection with others.

We can learn how to hold our concentration and awareness of each moment while being aware of our body, feelings, thoughts and environment. By "lingering longer" and focusing on our breath, we develop an awareness that not only reduces stress, but improves concentration.

Enhanced Relationships

Poet and civil rights activist Maya Angelou reminds us, "I've learned that people will forget what you said, people will forget what you did, but people will never forget how you made them feel."

On a regular basis, I am aware that my barometer for whether I enjoy or value interactions with others is tied to the feelings that ensue and remain after my connection. I recall a former colleague who was affirming, open and present every time we were together. I always felt valued and went away with warm feelings. I ask myself as well: Was I truly present for this person? Our simple presence speaks louder than words.

We are attracted to those who are most present for us. In today's world, it is sometimes painful to observe families at dinner or out in public. Instead of interacting with each other, they are interacting with their phones, which have captured their full attention.

Neuropsychologist Rick Hanson reminds us that with a mindful presence of others, we "become more settled into being fully there with them, more peacefully relaxed in awareness of them." Many of us have a tendency to get carried away by our thoughts and feelings and forget that the best gift we can give to another is the gift of our full presence.

Joy

One of my favorite books, *The Book of Joy*, by the 14th Dalai Lama and South African Anglican leader Desmond Tutu, reminds us, "In order to develop our mind, we must look at a deeper level. Everyone seeks happiness, joyfulness, but from outside—from money, from power, a nicer car, a bigger house. Most people never pay much attention to the Ultimate source of a happy life, which is inside, not outside."

In our busy world, we frequently miss the opportunity to enjoy the little pleasures that are happening now. It is easy to forget that what brings us joy is often in front of us. When we practice mindfulness, we learn to stop and calm so we can truly see a child's smile, a beautiful sky or a delicate spring flower. By lingering lovingly a little longer, the present moment is more likely to be embedded in our consciousness. So, as you practice, look into each experience more deeply and realize that you have all the conditions for happiness already available to you!

Peace

Today our peace and well-being are threatened by what we consume on a mental and emotional level. Social media and 24/7 news cycles bring the suffering of the world into our homes. This constant ingestion affects our thoughts and feelings, and often triggers old memories in our consciousness. It's necessary to stay informed, but sometimes limiting the information flow can be the first step to becoming more peaceful. In my recent book, *The Seeds of Love*, the quote on the cover reminds us, "That which we nurture in ourselves is that which we become."

The first step to peace can also be as simple as a smile. As Thich Nhat Hanh suggests, "If in our daily life we can smile, if we can be peaceful and happy, not only we, but everyone will profit from it." The Dalai Lama has said, "When we have inner peace, we can be at peace with those around us." To be peaceful requires a practice or a way of being that can break the cycle of violence and hatred so pervasive in many parts of our lives. The practice of mindfulness can help us discover the path to peace.

Mindfulness has relevance; learning to practice transforms our lives.

Mindfulness Test

To explore the concept of mindfulness, circle your responses to the following questions, which reflect some common barriers or blocks to mindfulness.

Barriers to Mindfulness

1. Do I suffer from "hurry sickness"? YES or NO
   This is a societal tendency to feel rushed and harried even when it is not necessary.

2. Do I measure happiness by anticipated future outcomes? YES or NO
   Evidence of this includes a preoccupation with thoughts such as, "I'll be happy when ..." "If only ..."

3. Do I constantly compare the present to the past? YES or NO
   This is the result of difficulty in letting go of experiences from the past, such as youth, summer, relationships, times of better health and so on.

4. Am I unwilling to confront the negative experiences in my life? Do I typically try to deny or push away pain? YES or NO

5. Do I have unfinished business in my life? Are there things that are incomplete that rob me of a sense of peace? Are there unexpressed feelings I have for others, perhaps a desire to forgive? Or unfulfilled aspirations, perhaps career or educational goals, travel adventures or experiences? YES or NO

6. Am I often bored with routines and normal day-to-day living? YES or NO
   Does life seem dull, and do I often find myself saying, "Another day of the same old thing"?

7. Is my life directed by old patterns or behaviors from the past? YES or NO
   These are long-held messages and behaviors you learned from family and society about how you should live your life.

Your responses to these questions provide a barometer of your patterns of mindfulness. Obviously, there is no perfect answer, and personal circumstances may dictate different responses. If you responded Yes to most of these questions, you may be missing opportunities for happiness. Becoming aware of your blocks and barriers to mindfulness offers you the freedom to enjoy each moment.

Contemplations

The flower, the sky, your beloved,
can only be found in the present moment.

—THICH NHAT HANH

For tomorrow, I offer no answers,
for yesterday I hold no apologies.
This moment is a gift which
I honor by fully living in it.

—MARY ANNE RADMACHER

Questions to Ponder

- Think of one stressful problem in your life. How might the practice of mindfulness help reduce your distress, and the negative consequences, of the problem?

- Explore areas in your life in which you are not as productive as you would like to be. How might the practice of mindfulness enhance concentration and productivity in your personal and professional life?

- Think of one person who you often take for granted. How might the practice of mindfulness bring new vitality to that relationship?

- What joyful moments in your life do you want to capture today?

- How can you create more peaceful moments in your life?

PART TWO
The Process

Our mind wanders, but our body's here and now, breathing. We can get dragged back into the past, which can lead to depression, or we can become anxious about the future which can lead to fear. Conscious breathing can be our anchor.
—**GARY GACH**

IN PART TWO YOU WILL

- Develop a technique for mindful breathing
- Learn a process for observing the mind and body
- Experience a mindfulness process

Mindful Breathing

Lessons on breathing were part of my early training in a doctorate program on health and psychology. By simply becoming aware of and changing my breathing pattern, I could regulate my body and mood. Later, I realized that this can be easily coupled with mindfulness practice, and I was empowered to go deeper.

Over the years I have had many opportunities to spend time in France at the Plum Village Retreat Center, at the time when it was the residence of Thich Nhat Hanh. At the entrance to the village, you are greeted by a large sign reading, "You have arrived. Enjoy breathing." In this peaceful community, mindfulness is practiced twenty-four hours a day, and breathing is at the heart of this practice. Any time a temple bell rings, or even an office or cell phone, people pause in their activities and bring their awareness back to their breath.

According to Thich Nhat Hanh, "Mindfulness is always being mindful of something." When we sit in meditation, we can become aware of our in-breath and out-breath. With a focus on the breath, we are able to bridge our mind, body and spirit, connecting the conscious and unconscious. All forms of meditation and mindfulness training begin with a focus on breathing. Breathing can offer us physical and mental equilibrium as well as inner harmony.

Most people breathe 17,000 to 24,000 breaths per day, yet few of us are aware of even one of those breathing cycles. Every moment our breath can create balance within us and bring us back to the present. Everything in nature rises, falls and exists. In the same way, inhalation is a rising, exhalation a falling, and the pause in between is the existing. We can learn to use our breathing as a metaphor for life and the balance that exists in all of nature.

Simply, our breath is a form of instant bio-feedback—this training doesn't require us to hook up to monitors. With each breath, we can learn ways in which we are holding stress and how we may be on alert as illustrated by chest breathing. To see if I am relaxed, I may place my hand on my abdomen to see if I am breathing deeply enough and in a relaxed state. When breathing from the chest we typically are on alert and abdominally we are relaxed. Watch a baby breathe; their natural rhythm is to breathe through their abdomen. They switch to chest breathing only when they are hungry or feeling discomfort. Likewise, as you become aware of your breathing, you will naturally slow down your breathing patterns and become aware of whether you are breathing more through your abdomen or diaphragm.

Finally, breathing offers one of the best ways to quiet the mind. A focus on breathing takes your attention away from your preoccupations. As philosopher and psychologist William James said, "The greatest weapon against stress is our ability to choose one thought over another." When you bring your full awareness to your breathing, you probably are not thinking about other concerns.

Mindful Breathing Practice

1. Find a comfortable sitting position, with your back straight.

Relax your hands and arms, or place them in your lap. Once you have learned this exercise, you may choose to keep your eyes either open or closed.

2. Bring your awareness to your breath. Do not change your breathing, but simply observe and experience the in and out movement of air through your nose or the rising and falling of your diaphragm. Connect the in-breath to the out-breath, the out-breath to the in-breath.

Note: To help you stay focused on the breath, you can repeat phrases or words. For example, as you breathe in and out you might repeat phrases such as:

Breathing in, I know that I am breathing in.
Breathing out, I know that I am breathing out.
or
Breathing in, I calm my body.
Breathing out, I smile.

Alternatively, you may choose to simply repeat a single word after each inhalation and exhalation, such as "in," "out," "calm" or "smile." Creating your own phrases or words may bring more meaning to your practice.

3. As you breathe, you will naturally become aware of thoughts, feelings, and bodily sensations. As you do, simply note them and then bring your attention back to your breath.

Learning to become aware of and observe your breathing is one of the best ways to learn mindfulness. As you will discover, an awareness of the breath makes it easier to focus on the moment, quiet the mind, and restore yourself. Discover for yourself the positive influence that breathing has on your own sense of balance and control. The Latin word for breath is "spiritus." Allow the breath to flow through you as a sense of spirit flows through your body.

In many Christian communities, the ringing of church bells often reminds the listeners to pause, pray and reflect, and in many parts of Asia, people pause in their activities at the sound of a temple bell. One of the best ways to practice mindful breathing is to stop and pause to break the cycle of doing, going and frenetic activity. After becoming aware of this practice, I purchased a small bell. The bell sits in a prominent location, ready to be rung by anyone passing by. The sound of the bell is then a reminder to each person in the house to stop, pause and take a deep slow breath.

In a university class on mindfulness, I once asked my students, "Besides a bell, what else could be used as a reminder to stop and breathe?" A deaf student responded, "My six-month-old baby is like a bell of mindfulness. I pause and hold her and realize how precious she and this moment are."

Ten Breaths

Gary Schneider, in his book *Ten Breaths to Happiness*, reminds us that conscious breathing does not take a lot a time to do. It simply means bringing your mind back to your body. Freedom is available when we come back to the present moment. By simply focusing on our breathing for ten breaths we can change the neural pathways in the brain. Instead of focusing on habitual patterns of anger and fear, we can focus on mindful breathing—for Ten Breaths. According to Thich Nhat Hanh, this can develop the habit energy of happiness.

Contemplations

Our habits are strong, so a certain discipline is required to step outside our cocoon and receive the magic of our surroundings. Pause practice—taking three conscious breaths at any moment when we notice that we are stuck—is a simple but powerful practice that each of us can do at any given moment.

—PEMA CHODRON

Breathing in, I am aware that I am breathing in.
Breathing out, I am aware that I am breathing out.
Breathing in, I am grateful for this moment.
Breathing out, I smile Breathing in,
I am aware of the preciousness of this day.
Breathing out, I vow to live deeply in this day.

—THICH NHAT HANH

Questions to Ponder

- Can you identify daily situations where you might use breathing to come back to the present moment, to renew yourself, and to quiet your mind?

- How might you use bells in your life to remind you and others to pause, breathe and enjoy the moment? Since bells are a metaphor, what else could represent a bell of mindfulness in your life? A stoplight? The ringing of a cell phone? A bird song?

The Mindfulness Journey

The curious paradox is that when I accept myself just as I am, then I can change.

—CARL ROGERS

A famous meditation teacher was once asked, "How long do you meditate each day?" The reply was, "Formally, for several hours per day I sit and meditate, and informally I meditate all day long, with every activity becoming the focus of my meditation." Saint Paul, a Christian apostle, was once asked how long he prayed every day. His reply was similar: "I pray for several hours each day; however, I hope my life is a prayer." Learning to become more mindful is not about creating a constantly blissful state. It is about being present for every activity and every relationship. It is the process of being awake to life.

The practice of mindfulness is often sabotaged by various interruptions and distractions. For example, how many times during your day do you find yourself thinking about the upcoming weekend? Or how often do you allow your phone to hijack what you are currently doing? These distractions—include our senses and they put our bodies are in a state of constant physiological change, evoking muscular tension, breathing rate, comfort and pain.

Sometimes people ask: What are the qualities that make up the present moment? I often call this the "anatomy of the present moment." You may be intrigued to realize that much more is going on in each moment than you ever realized. With that awareness, you learn what is happening in the present moment without allowing yourself to be transfixed and carried away by these sensations.

Scanning NOW

The following process offers a deep exploration into the present moment. To discover the nuances of this moment, begin by finding a comfortable place to sit, where you will be free of distractions for the period of time you have available. With your awareness focused on the *in* and *out* of your breath, begin—without judgment and with patience—to explore your body, feelings and thoughts, and the story you have created. Explore as if you were a beginner attempting to learn more about yourself. Allow yourself to read slowly and discover ...

Bodily Experiences

Every moment lived in awareness offers information regarding changes going on within your body. Note for a moment how your breathing changes. Recognize areas of discomfort or pain, most often reflected in muscular tension. Become aware of any temperature shifts between warmth and coolness in various parts of your body. What are you experiencing in your body at this moment? Notice and label that sensation. For example, label tightness in the neck and shoulders as "tension." Experience the sensation fully, and then return to your breath.

Now include an awareness of your primary senses: seeing, hearing, tasting, smelling and touching. Look around you. What do you see? Notice every sound within your body and in your surroundings. What do you hear? What do you smell at this moment? "Braille" (touch) your immediate environment.

As you gradually become more aware of your bodily sensations, you literally are "coming to your senses" and enhancing your potential for becoming more mindful.

Feelings

Thoughts and sensations create within us a variety of feelings that are pleasant, unpleasant or neutral. Pleasant feelings, such as joy, gratitude and peacefulness, often enhance the mindfulness process. It is easy to be present for exciting and happy moments. Unpleasant feelings, such as anger and sadness, are often avoided. Neutral feelings are typical during times of boredom or periods during which nothing pleasant or unpleasant arises. Notice what you are feeling at this moment. Are your feelings pleasant, unpleasant or neutral? What specific feelings are you experiencing? Notice and label what you perceive and feel.

Perceptions and Thoughts

What am I thinking now? What kind of thoughts are most frequent? Note the beginning of a thought and its middle, and then follow the thought to its end. Thoughts and small children have one thing in common: They need attention! Recognize what happens to your thoughts as you simply notice and label each one as "thinking," and then return to your breath.

Our thoughts are so powerful that they can quickly turn into ideas or judgments about ourselves and others. We might ask ourselves the question, "Am I sure?" Our perceptions are often inaccurate. Can you recall a situation in which you created a view about something or someone that turned out to be totally false? Inaccurate perceptions can form when thoughts become distorted.

Mental Formations: Stories of Our Life

Our perceptions of our experiences are formed over time by ever-changing experiences and interactions. If you look back at your life, you will find that because of the myriad of experiences, both positive and negative, you have formed a story that you continue to repeat. It's easy for us to become annoyed by hearing the same repeated story in others. "My mother and father were too busy for me." Or, "If only I had a better education like my sister." When we hear this again and again from a friend, we become annoyed. Needless to say, we repeat our own stories about our lives, and often they are also negative and judgmental.

Overall, it is clear that our bodies keep score. Bessel Van der Kolk, a neuroscience researcher "shows that the only way we can change the way we feel is by becoming aware of our inner experience and learning to befriend what is going inside ourselves." He suggests that we tally all the experiences of our life both positive and negative, which are markers for our mental health and our ability to be with others.

Three Easy Ways to Begin a Practice: Stop, Calm and Look Deeply

To cultivate a practice of returning to the present moment, consider ways in which you can stop, calm and look deeply at the phenomena of the present moment. This can be done by taking pauses as short as three to ten conscious breaths for renewal. Gradually, you can extend this process to longer periods of time.

Stopping

The first step in any type of meditation—the key to developing mindfulness—is learning how to stop. In stopping, we let go of the past and future and dwell on what is happening in the present moment. Each day offers many opportunities to cultivate the art of stopping—connecting with people remind us to be present. I installed an app on my computer that sounds a bell randomly, so I am reminded to pause and breathe. Taking an entire day to stop and such as a Sabbath or Shabbat. When I was growing up, Sunday was offered as a day of rest. Our family often gathered, and we felt a sense of renewal. In Buddhist mindfulness communities, we welcome "lazy days," where we practice *being* rather than *doing*. This refreshing practice offers respite from a busy world.

Calming

One of the most powerful ways to strengthen the "muscle" of our attention is to return our focus, again and again throughout the day, to what we are doing. The 17th-century mystic Saint Francis de Sales said, "Even if you bring yourself back thousands of times, it will be worth it." When we focus on something repetitively—such as our breathing, mantras or phrases, or prayers—or when we become truly present for a pet or a friend, we strengthen our ability to find inner calm. We can also find internal peace through meditation.

Looking Deeply

When you stop and calm, you learn how to become more relaxed and mindful in the present moment. Concentration is cultivated, allowing you to look deeply and understand the source of your current feelings and perceptions, and the stories you have created about your life or others. When we stop, calm and look deeply with a loved one who is suffering, we may begin to get a glimpse of why they are experiencing pain. From this understanding comes love.

If you want to make mindfulness a part of your life, practice is required. You need to allow yourself time for this simple and beautiful process. I prefer to begin my day with a short period to stop and focus on my breathing. During your day, simply remember from time to time to focus on your breath. Remember to come back to each moment. Eventually, you will become aware of ways to apply mindfulness to all the moments of your life.

Contemplations

We might begin by scanning our body ... and then asking, "What is happening?" We might also ask, "What wants my attention right now?" or, "What is asking for acceptance?"

—TARA BRACH

If mindfulness refers to keeping one's consciousness alive to the present reality, then one must practice right now in one's daily life, not only during meditation sessions.

—THICH NHAT HANH

Questions to Ponder

- How can the process of stopping, calming and looking deeply bring you to a deeper understanding of yourself and your relationships?
- In what circumstances, both personally and professionally, might you apply this mindfulness process to your life?

PART THREE
Applications

The mind is like water. When it's turbulent, it's difficult to see. When it's calm, everything becomes clear. —**HEENA PATEL**

IN PART THREE YOU WILL

- Discover how to quiet the mind
- Engage in a process of transforming feelings

Quieting the Mind

During several trips to rural parts of India, I was always fascinated by the number of monkeys leaping from branch to branch through the trees. After having lunch with our tour group, one member said, "Oh, that is where the phrase "monkey mind" comes from!" The Buddha coined the term to remind his students that their minds were like monkeys, leaping from one thought to another.

Many people feel uncomfortable when it is quiet. They seem more comfortable when the TV is on or the radio is playing, or they are responding to their phone or are busy with activities. I often ask people, "What is the one way you quiet your mind?" Their responses are varied and usually include activities such as music, exercise, watching movies or reading—all activities which can be pleasurable and relaxing and can *also* be a form of distraction or diversion. It seems clear that "busyness," as we know it, is often a bypass and possibly related to not wanting to experience what is really going on in our inner lives.

Many of us have discovered that quieting the mind happens naturally when we get away from our hectic environments. The office and home environment are not always conducive to becoming peaceful.

Going out into nature often facilitates a natural quieting of the mind and body. No special technique is needed. All you need to do to merge with the rhythm of nature is to put on your walking shoes and take a hike in the forest or a walk in a local park or on the beach. Research shows that people who have access to natural settings experience better health. I have discovered that only a few hours of being in nature brings peace, and a deep sense of relaxation and harmony is restored. We evolved in a way that was more closely connected with nature, and I suspect this ease and comfort are part of our natural state.

For those who have the time to get away, attending a meditation retreat can be restorative. After several days of silence at a retreat, I often discover things about myself that I never recognized before. During my first ten-day silent retreat, I found myself unexpectedly crying during a meditation session. It was clear that once I stopped, calmed and let go of my busyness I could find a natural catharsis. This cleansing seems to happen more in solitude and quiet. With other demands on the side, I was more likely to be connected to past fears and traumas. In my running days, I recall running alone in the mountains and at times tears would arise. Research suggests the shedding of emotional tears (different than onions) releases oxytocin and endorphins. This natural release only comes when the mind is quiet.

A major source of stress is how the mind interprets situations in our lives. Most of our stress originates from thoughts about the past or concerns about the future. Our bodies respond physiologically as we obsess about what has already happened or what might happen. Many people are troubled with such thoughts at bedtime or in the middle of the night, when our mental stories can loom larger than life, and our preoccupation with the past or future results in insomnia. Living in the present is difficult, but we might want to reflect on how many times we have become preoccupied with the potential disasters of some event in the future, only to realize when the time finally arrived that most of our worrying was in vain.

One of my favorite contemplations comes from the words of Mark Twain:

> *I am an old man and have known a great many troubles, but most of them never happened. Worrying is like paying a debt you don't owe. I have spent most of my life worrying about things that have never happened. Drag your thoughts away from your troubles ... by the ears, by the heels, or any other way you can manage it.*

Clearly, it is important to plan for the future, but not to be obsessed with outcomes. In planning, it is human nature to consider all possible negative consequences or worst-case scenarios. However, according to cognitive therapists, the mind has a tendency to create "cognitive distortions." These mental distortions and preoccupations with the past or the future become invitations to live outside the present moment. But more significantly, these thoughts become the basis for stress and anxiety. Learning to quiet the mind is the basis for becoming more mindful and more open to the beauty surrounding us.

There are many techniques for quieting the mind. Most techniques focus on a word, phrase, sound or object—such as the flame of a candle—to help us become more focused and centered. The following technique places emphasis on labeling thoughts. This strategy may be helpful for those who have difficulty falling asleep or are obsessing about worries.

Quieting the Mind: Basic Practice

Since most distress relates to a preoccupation with thoughts, practice observing these thoughts and then letting go of them.

1. Begin to focus on your breath at the tip of your nostrils or on the rising and falling of the abdomen. Keep your attention on the breath.

2. Naturally, thoughts will arise. Use these thoughts as the object of your meditation. Simply become aware of them and note their general nature. You might label the thought as one of hunger, pain, sleep or sex, for example.

3. Bring your attention back to your breath. Through simple awareness of the thought, it loses some of its power. Do not resist the thought, since what you resist persists. Learn to witness in a detached way the thoughts will gradually pass. Thought as like clouds they come and go!

4. When the mind is quiet, the body is quiet. When the body is quiet, the mind is quiet. Learning to quiet your mind is one of the most basic ways to become relaxed and peaceful.

Contemplations

Within each of us there is a silence—a silence as vast as a universe. We are afraid of it ... and we long for it.

—**GUNILLA NORRIS**

Questions to Ponder

- Take a few breaths and a moment to reflect: Is there one predominant worry that dominates your awareness?

- Sometimes people use the metaphor of keeping our minds like a "clear blue sky." This mindset would be ideal, and yet we know that clouds come and go. Look deeply; what are the sources of some of your troubling mental clouds?

- Can you identify situations in which you can use the "quieting the mind" technique? For example, the technique was helpful to me several times while writing this book. I discovered that my worries about getting my work to the editor would get in the way of clarifying a point or staying with the theme of the present chapter. By taking a moment to label my thoughts ("hurry thought") and then breathe, I was typically able to quickly bring myself back to the task at hand.

- Using a "beginner's mind," take some time to explore the nature of your thoughts. Can you trace the beginning and end of each thought as you sit quietly? What types of thoughts are you experiencing? Can you recognize that they are only mental formations?

Transforming Feelings

If you don't transform, you will transmit.

—THICH NHAT HANH

When we reflect on the fabric of our lives, we recall memories and moments that frame the quality of our lives Memories stem from positive or negative experiences that can continue to influence our current overall mood, and sometimes add a depth of understanding. Often, we recall the cherished moment and usually never forget the challenging ones. Typically, the more emotionally charged the situation, the longer the memory stays with us.

This chapter will help you become aware of and explore your experiences as they arise. We can learn how to embrace and be more alive to our emotions, even when they are challenging emotions such as fear or anger. Every day our feelings—positive, negative or neutral—wake us up or lull us into a state of complacency. Learning to *be* with each of these feelings is the essence of mindfulness. As the poet Rumi says in "The Guest House":

This being human is a guest house.
Every morning a new arrival.

A joy, a depression, a meanness,
some momentary awareness comes
as an unexpected visitor.
Welcome and entertain them all! …

Fear

Fear is a powerful emotion that alerts us to risk or danger. The limbic system is hard-wired for fight or flight, making fear an emotion that can save our life. But many of our fears are irrational. Our modern-day fears, which can even be strong enough to keep us awake at night, often center around relationships and acceptance. It is common to relieve situations that happened the previous day, and fear becomes alive when we question *am I enough*? *Or did I act properly*? *Why did I say that*?

I have often spent time questioning previous decisions, but much of what I feared was irrational and distorted. We can use an acronym to help us understand the word: **FEAR** is **F**alse **E**vidence **A**ppearing **R**eal. So many of our fears are irrational or distorted and therapies have been developed such as originally Rational Emotive Therapy and more recently Mindfulness Based Cognitive Therapy.

Anger

We all have received a variety of messages about how to deal with anger. For some of us, the expression of anger was punished or frowned upon. My mother seemed to have some sayings when she sensed I was angry such as "I'll show you something to be angry about" and "Gerald, be nice." For others, anger is seen as a healthy means of venting feelings of pain or grief and eliminating stress.

Working with Feelings

Name It

In *A Path with Heart*, Jack Kornfield shares, "In ancient cultures shamans learned that to name that which they feared was a practical way to begin to have power over it." Once I give this feeling a name, it seems to demystify it and make it feel more benign. Naming an emotion can also make it seem less confusing. I like to call my feeling by its real name, "Hello fear!" And then I ask, "What is that you are asking me to look at in my life?"

Be with Your Feeling—Tea with Mara!

One of my favorite stories from the time of the Buddha was about his visits with Mara, a demon god who represented anger and other challenging emotions. Mara often visited the Buddha and Ananda, the Buddha's attendant, was always on alert. One night, Ananda saw Mara and expressed uncertainty about what to do. Instead of trying to banish Mara, the Buddha told him, "Invite Mara for tea!" The Buddha believed that even an evil spirit can be transformed, just as compost becomes beautiful flowers. Learning to stay with challenging emotions helps us deepen our understanding of ourselves.

Embrace and Replace

The best antidote to fear is learning to embrace it and then replace it with love. This is what the Buddha suggested to the 500 visiting monks when they were afraid to mediate in the forest. They heard frightening sounds that they assumed were bad spirits. When they shared their fears with the Buddha, he taught them the Loving-kindness Meditation (see the "Metta Practice" below). In this meditation, one replaces the challenging feeling, such as fear, with love.

Linger Longer with Positive Feelings

That which we nurture in ourselves is that which we become. Learning to discover where we place our focus in life is a gift of this practice. Challenging emotions need our attention, so they are not transmitted, and the positive feelings need to be nurtured so they grow. The more we focus on qualities such as kindness, compassion and joy, the more these qualities will manifest in ourselves. In a similar way, when we linger longer with a person or beautiful nature scene, we imprint that memory in our consciousness.

Transforming Feelings: Basic Practice

To transform a feeling, begin with mindful breathing. Focus on your breath at the tip of your nostrils or the abdomen. Keep your attention on the breath as it flows in and out. Naturally, thoughts, such as anger, will enter your consciousness and may lead to an emotional state. Any challenging feeling—jealousy, doubt, sadness or guilt—can be used in this practice. As the feeling enters your consciousness, simply become aware of it, and then bring your attention back to your breath. When you offer simple awareness to the feeling, it loses some of its power.

In this moment, accept the feeling. Do not resist it. Rather, embrace it. Befriend your anger and become one with it. As you breathe in and breathe out, observe and study the feeling. Begin to calm the anger through your mindful breathing and the repetition of verses, such as this phrase used at the Plum Village Retreat Center:

Experiencing the feeling of anger in me, I breathe in.
Smiling at the feeling of anger in me, I breathe out.

Preferably, create your own short phrases, and repeat and connect them with each breathing cycle. Here are some examples:

Breathing in, I recognize my anger.
Breathing out, I am aware of how angry I am.
Breathing in, I see my anger overwhelming me.
Breathing out, I recognize that the anger
affects my entire body.

Through continued awareness and the cultivation of calmness, you will find it becomes easier to change the intensity of the anger and gradually release it.

Practice Metta

Metta, or loving-kindness, is a practice that can easily be incorporated into our lives. It is like a prayer that we offer first to ourselves, then to someone we have empathy for or are fond of, and then to someone we feel neutral towards or even someone who is challenging. We practice offering loving-kindness with the purpose of creating happiness in another person or other people, as well as ourselves. Metta is the process of developing compassionate energy, which literally infuses our every interaction.

Sometimes it seems easier to share loving-kindness with others than to remember to include ourselves in the process. Many of us grew up with the admonition that we must put others first, sometimes at the expense of loving ourselves. But how is it possible to give others what we have not nurtured in ourselves? Personally, I have discovered that practicing loving-kindness toward myself through meditation, quiet reflection, long walks and, above all, time with loved ones, provides me more time and energy to give to others; ultimately, everyone benefits.

During the practice of Metta, we direct loving-kindness to ourselves. We then extend thoughts of loving-kindness to others by repeating phrases of goodwill and blessing, replacing the "I" with "you." We conclude by sending this loving-kindness to people we love and, often, to those who we know are struggling.

Metta Phrases

May I be filled with loving-kindness.
May I be safe.
May I be healthy.
May I have ease of body and mind.
May I be at peace.
(Repeat: May I, you, we and all)

Contemplations

Our deepest fears are like dragons,
guarding our deepest treasures.

—RAINER MARIA RILKE

Hanging onto resentment is letting someone
you despise live rent-free in your head

—ESTHER LEDERER

Questions to Ponder

- Think of one feeling you typically have difficulty with, and then allow yourself some time to practice the basic technique for transforming feelings described in this chapter. After completing this practice session, take some time to write about your experience. Note: How you are feeling in this moment?

- In what ways, do you resist your feelings as they arise? Resistance may even occur through keeping overly busy or losing yourself on social media.

PART FOUR
The Mindful Life

Aware of the suffering caused by unmindful consumption, I am committed to cultivating good health, both physical and mental, for myself, my family, and my society by practicing mindful eating, drinking, and consuming. I will practice looking deeply into my consumption of the Four Kinds of Nutriments—edible foods, sense impressions [media and news], volition, and consciousness. —**THICH NHAT HANH**

IN PART FOUR YOU WILL

- Explore the joy of mindful eating
- Become aware of your media consumption
- Explore the practice of mindful walking
- Discover the essence of loving relationships

Mindful Consumption

The preceeding quote is from the Five Mindfulness Trainings, the ethical basis for practicing mindfulness in the Thich Nhat Hanh tradition. Although these trainings have a Buddhist origin, they were written with secular implications. Especially in today's world, we realize that consumption is not merely what we eat and drink; it also relates to all that we consume through our senses, including social media, news, books and movies. This influences our perceptions and views, which then easily become imprinted in our consciousness—which contains everything we have experienced during our lifetime. This also illustrates the way in which we use consumption of all kinds to push away our problems rather than deal with them.

This chapter focuses on both mindful eating and the consumption of media. Both can have healing influences as well as negative consequences.

Mindful Eating

Mindful eating replaces self-criticism with self-nurturing. It replaces shame with respect for your own inner wisdom

—**JAN CHOZEN BAY**

When mindfulness is applied to eating, it becomes a powerful tool that can enhance the joy and beneficial effects of food. Eating is all too frequently a mindless activity; we gulp our meals down and combine them with other activities, such as reading the newspaper, checking our phone and watching television. Often families or couples come together to enjoy a meal, but the center of attention is their phones. Eating becomes a secondary experience, and its real pleasure is often missed. Research on eating shows that mindless consumption of food is linked to binge eating and emotional eating. When we are stressed, a sweet roll sometimes offers a temporary lift, but this strategy for alleviating stress can cause weight gain.

For many, preparing for a meal includes gathering to say a prayer before the first bite. My family always offered a traditional Catholic prayer. We began with the sign of the cross and then rushed through the recitation. After becoming aware of the practice of mindfulness, I was asked to say grace at my mother's funeral. I invoked the sign of the cross slowly and with care. Then I went on to say, "Bless us, O Lord, and these, thy gifts ... (I paused and opened my hands to the table of food) ... which we (I made eye contact with the group) are about to receive from thy bounty. Through Christ, our Lord. Amen." It took me twice as long to recite the prayer, but for the first time, I felt the true meaning of the words. Try this with your version of grace, as a way to help everyone gather before a meal or to center yourself if you are dining solo. Being grateful is a wonderful way to start a meal.

When we are about to begin a meal, a few simple reminders may add to pleasure and meaning to the act of eating:

- Take a moment to reflect on the food that you are about to receive as a gift from the Earth.

- Imagine the laborers who made this meal. For example, when I eat rice, I sometimes recall seeing women in Vietnam bending over muddy rice paddies as they tended the young plants.

- Take the time to express gratitude for those who prepared the meal and for those who might be sharing the meal with you.

- Consider the habit energy you may have around food. Do you eat too fast? Too much? How might you be more mindful about your consumption?

- Reflect on the environmental footprint your food created before it reached your table. When we consume, how may we reduce harm to animals, plants and our precious Earth?

- Reflect on the blessing of your food, and how the meal will support your body and lifestyle.

Mindful Eating Process

- Before eating, remember your purpose: *to eat*.

- Before eating, take a moment to become aware of your breathing.

- Slow down the overall eating process. Chew your food slowly.

- Involve all your senses—sight, hearing, taste, smell and touch—as you experience your food.

- When your mind wanders, bring your awareness back to the moment. Make taste, sensation and gratitude the focus of your attention.

You will find that mindful eating makes mealtimes more gratifying experiences. For some people, becoming mindful about their eating process may be one of the best underlying strategies for weight control. Food that is chewed slowly is easily digested, and you are less likely to overeat.

Think about your last meal. Can you recall the various tastes, smells and textures that you experienced? Try an experiment in mindful eating, using an orange. Take the orange and slowly peel it, enjoying the fragrance released from the peel. Do you begin to salivate before you actually taste the orange? Carefully divide the orange into sections and eat one small piece at a time. What do you notice as the orange touches your lips and tongue? Try this same experiment with a partner whose eyes are closed. Slowly feed the orange to your partner, and notice how all the senses are involved in the process of taste.

Mindful Media Consumption

In many situations, we have a choice as to what kind of images and sounds we allow into our awareness. My wife and I recently went out to our favorite theatre to see an inspiring biography. For 15 minutes, our senses were assaulted during previews that were mostly violent. They created a mood that we had to shake off just before we watched this wonderful movie—quite a paradox.

If we consume too much negative media, it is easy to have this kind of assault 24-7. By following the news cycle, it is easy to be in a state of arousal and anxiety caused by the fear it generates. My personal practice is to protect my mental and emotional state by nurturing the positive qualities or seeds such as love and happiness, while limiting the contamination of seeds that incite fear and anger, or that trigger negative memories in my consciousness.

I find that with the plethora of media today, I have to be selective in what I allow into my consciousness. I have learned that consuming too much news or social media with a negative message influences my attitude and mood for longer periods of time. More importantly, I am aware that my feelings influence my consciousness. When I focus on consuming books, articles and movies that inspire and create feelings of happiness, my spiritual and psychological growth is enhanced. What we consume is who we become!

Author, Buddhist and media scholar Holly Stocking offers some guidance for consuming the news and other media. She suggests that we begin to apply mindfulness "by consuming the news slowly, observing any afflicted emotions that come up and then bringing the mind back to love and compassion and nonattachment."

Next, ask yourself these questions:

Does anger arise?

One barometer for determining the impact of news and social media is related to the anger that often arises. I continue to discover that my anger is often based on my bias and lack of understanding toward those with a different view.

Am I able to listen to both sides of the news and to others who have a different view?
Most of our suffering is related to a dualistic view that automatically pits one side against the other. What would it be like if I listened to family members and friends who hold different views? Would some understanding surface and replace any angry feelings which can easily shadow what is true?

Does fear or despair arise?
Often when fear or despair arise, we are hijacked by the feelings. Instead, we could take a moment to pause and consider small actions that may make a difference. Recently, I was aware of my communications and feelings that arose during a discussion about politics with a relative. Although we both agreed not to talk politics, yet it was clear we each had our own views. Instead of talking about differences, we decided to focus on all the wonderful things we have in common. Looking deeper, we instead now share more meaningful events and the core of love that always united us.

Relieve our cynicism
We sometimes feel cynical about the news and certain media networks and begin to stereotype those who hold views that conflict with our own. Instead of having a face-to-face or phone conversation, it is easy to continue an email debate, missing an opportunity to understand the other.

Cynicism can even arise in helping professionals as they work with those who are suffering. Noted teacher and author Joan Halifax observed how helping professionals suffer from "empathetic distress," which has a completely draining and debilitating effect. When we identify too much with those who are suffering—such as working as a caregiver—we may mirror those we are trying to help. Although, we automatically see empathy as positive, yet too much causes distress. When noticing the pain in ourselves and others, it is "registered in the neural networks in our brains, associated with pain. Whereas the compassion phase of working with others registered in neural networks associated with positive emotions."

This seems to be true when a person is overly invested in the media. Overconsumption of negative news, combined with our own direct contact with pain and suffering, may induce not only cynical and depressing feelings; it can also have greater ramifications in how these events are recorded in our brains. Simply, the more news we consume, especially when it creates feelings of fear and anger, the more likely it will rewire neural pathways in our brains that are not conducive to well-being.

Ultimately, with our consumption we are often trying to address unmet needs. There are reasons, for example, that people overeat or obsess about their social media feed. According to social media expert Doug Firebaugh, we log on for "acknowledgment, attention, approval, appreciation, acclaim, assurance and inclusion." What needs are not being met in your life that lead you to consuming in ways that are not healthy?

Contemplations

When was the last time you had a glass of water and really drank it?

—THOMAS MERTON

Mindful eating is a way to become reacquainted with the guidance of our internal nutritionist.

—JAN CHOZEN BAYS

Every time you spend money, you're casting a vote for the kind of world you want.

—ANNA LAPPÉ

You are on the footsteps of whom you follow. As you have to be cautious when you choose your friends, you have to be cautious when you choose who to follow on social media.

—ASMAA DOKMAK

If social media controls you and is robbing you of your freedom and good emotional energy, chances are you're addicted and it's time to find another hobby.

—GERMANY KENT

Questions to Ponder

- In what ways may I bring mindfulness to eating?
- Do I find myself eating for emotional benefits? To fulfill a need?
- In what ways does social media and news consume my life? What might I do with the extra time?
- What are the conditions that are needed for my happiness now?
- What is the difference between my needs and wants?

Mindful Walking

When we walk slowly, the world can fully appear. Not only are the creatures not frightened away by our haste or aggression, but the fine detail of fern and flower, or devastation and disruption, becomes visible.

—JOAN HALIFAX

To walk mindfully is to meditate while you walk. Think how much time you spend walking on a daily basis. Typically, the purpose of your walking is to go somewhere, to arrive. Because of "hurry sickness" or a lack of awareness, we often miss the real journey. Recalling hikes and walks I've taken in the past, I believe my main purpose was always to arrive somewhere, and when I was walking with another person, I wanted to arrive first! Learning to walk mindfully is not as easy as it seems. The idea is to walk and enjoy the walking itself. That means learning to focus on the *walking* and not on the *destination*.

When you practice walking meditation, you go for a stroll. You have no purpose or direction in space or time. The purpose of walking meditation is walking meditation itself. Going is important, not arriving. Each step is peace and joy.

—THICH NHAT HANH

Mindful Walking Process

1. Recall your purpose in this moment: *to walk.*

2. Stop and observe: Where is my attention?

3. Become aware of your breathing. Focus on the in-breath and the out-breath.

4. Begin walking with your left foot, and while breathing in say, "In." As your right foot moves forward, breathe out and say, "Out." Vary your pace and breathing to suit your needs and the environment.

5. As your mind wanders, bring your awareness back to the moment by breathing in and breathing out as you move.

When walking indoors, your pace will be slower, usually one or two steps for each in-breath and the same for each out-breath. Outdoors, coordinate your breathing with your steps. You may find that three or four steps per in-breath and out-breath may be suitable for you. Using the words, "In, in, in, out, out, out," can help you to stay focused.

Having read this section and perhaps even tried some mindful walking, you may think this process might be rather tedious or frustrating. Think about what you may experience along the journey that you previously have missed. Flowers, trees, wind, sky, children laughing, raindrops on the pavement, intriguing architecture, the smiles of others. A new world opens up to you, and as it does, stop, pause, and enjoy each scene, sound, smell and experience along the way. Breathe! Continue your focus on walking.

I recall a hike with my son to a beautiful mountain peak. We talked all the way to the top. One solid hour of walking and talking. He decided that on the way down we would walk mindfully without talking. Later, reflecting on that hike, we both commented on how we became closer as father and son, sharing thoughts and feelings while we walked up the mountain. We also recognized how many more flowers, birds and trees we saw or heard on the way down. The journey up the mountain created moments of intimacy between a father and son. The journey down the mountain created intimacy between father, son, mountain and nature.

Opportunities to Begin a Practice of Mindful Walking

1. One of the easiest ways to begin this practice is to attend a retreat, "day of mindfulness" or prayer group. This way your practice will be supported by the energy and pace of the group.

2. Try walking at varied speeds. I recall being on a retreat in a monastery in China, where the walking pace varied depending on the ability of participants. Various circles formed and the outer circle walked like race walkers. Each circle going inward would walk at a slower pace. Often the older monks would be walking in a smaller inner circle.

3. Join a regular walking group—this often brings us closer to nature and each other—the best way to sustain the practice.

4. Find ways to walk mindfully while at work. No one even needs to know you are practicing as you enjoy an infor-

mal stroll down the hallway. Often, I will walk indoors around our small house as a break to my sedentary writer's routine.

5. Vary your form and try "retro walking," or backward walking. I first learned this exercise during Tai Chi sessions in a park in China. This form is good for both your mind and your body. It offers cardiovascular benefits and since the muscles and joints work in different ways it can improve your balance. Recently, my physical therapist recommended this form, and now I often walk backward on hills in our neighborhood and feel the restorative benefit. Warning: This may prompt some strange stares. This is especially true for me when walking my dog. But I find walking this way to be one of the best ways to enhance mindfulness while moving. The brain recognizes this as a completely different activity, which creates heightened attention.

Walking is a barometer of how mindfully we are living our life. I'm learning that being mindful of my posture offers an awareness of my overall well-being. Do I find myself leaning forward or in a hurry? I like the mantra, "walking with no place to go." The journey is the practice, which is the heart of mindfulness. While walking, I remind myself to put a smile between my shoulders and relax. Walking reminds us to connect with the Earth, while offering gratitude for the ability to physically move. As we walk with care, we bring peace to ourselves and offer a symbol of peace for others.

Contemplations

Take my hand. We will walk. We will only walk. We will enjoy our walk without thinking of arriving anywhere. Walk peacefully. Walk happily. Our walk is a peace walk. Our walk is a happiness walk.

—THICH NHAT HANH

But the beauty is in the walking—we are betrayed by destinations.

—GWYN THOMAS

The contemplative dimension of walking comes through my presence to the world around me and to what is moving through me as I walk.

—CHRISTINE VALTERS PAINTNER

Questions to Ponder

Explore ways in which mindfulness is enhanced with every step you take. Consider opportunities for more mindful walking and use each step as a means of coming back to the present moment. Think about your typical walking patterns.

- What does your way of walking say about you?

- If your steps could talk, what would they say?

- Looking from a greater perspective, are the steps you are taking in your life today a message you want to leave for others?

Loving Relationships

True love comes from an understanding and practice of loving-kindness, compassion, joy and equanimity.

—THICH NHAT HANH

With mindfulness, you will learn a new language to explore the true meaning of love. You'll also learn that love is more than a feeling; it requires action. The qualities of loving-kindness, compassion, joy and equanimity are essential to all relationships. When we explore these qualities, we discover the best ways to create the understanding necessary to really love another.

Loving-Kindness

What would our relationships be like if we were always mindful of an intention to offer others happiness? When we practice loving-kindness, our sole intention is to make every interaction an opportunity for keeping goodwill for others foremost in our heart. We have a calligraphy poster in our home by Thich Nhat Hanh that says, "How may I best love you?" This has been a mantra for us as we continue to find new ways to support and love one another.

A practice in small African villages begins with the naming of a baby before it is conceived. The couple creates a name, coupled with a song, and they sing it to each other as they are making love. Once the baby is born, the couple and community sing that song to the child as he or she grows older, and it becomes the child's song. The child grows and continues through life, and at their death and beyond they are known and remembered by their song. We have a picture in our home with the inscription, "My beloved knows my song and sings it when I forget." This is another way to remember the ways that we may best love those who are important in our lives.

Being mindful of the other creates understanding and love. With this awareness, we look at what and who we love in different ways. We learn to first love ourselves unconditionally. The late Rabbi Israel Friedlander talked about the biblical commandment, "Love your neighbor as yourself." He said we focus on the first part of the injunction, and yet we should equally love ourselves so we can truly love our neighbor.

With the insight of loving-kindness, we do all that is possible so that others in our lives feel joy. This I find happens with those we know the best and, hopefully, with those we are in relationship with. It is also a quality that some people naturally exude; you may experience this quality in a caregiver, barista or store employee, and sometimes after merely a short contact with another. The employees in the stores and coffee shops I patronize often exude loving-kindness.

Practices to Develop Loving-Kindness

1. **Understand who and what we love.** Mindfulness is about remembering who we are and what we love. The practice of loving-kindness begins with an intention or direction for our love. Taking time to reflect on the questions, "What do I love?" and "Who do I love?" will support the beginning of understanding how best to love.

2. **Be love.** It is easy to expect others to be loving and kind, but often the mutuality of this concept is forgotten. Learning to take care of our self as a parent, partner and co-worker demonstrates the kind of self-love that is necessary for renewal and well-being. When a parent takes time to nurture her or himself, she models a positive message of self-care and love that cannot be replaced with words. Being a model or a messenger of loving-kindness is always the best way to ultimately receive love ourselves.

Compassion

Compassion arises from the boundless nature of love. If we are truly practicing loving-kindness, we want the best for others and want to relieve their suffering. Compassion is the intention and capacity to relieve the sorrows of another and transform suffering. The word compassion has two aspects. "Com" means to be with the suffering, and "passion" means to lighten the load of another.

Several years ago, my wife and I accompanied a group of students on a pilgrimage to India. On this journey, and from the vantage point of an elevated tour bus, we were all deeply moved by the sight of a young girl, about six years old, with a severe facial deformity. We later learned that a large tumor, growing inside her mouth from birth, caused many challenges, especially malnutrition, as well as psychological burdens for her and her family. After our journey, our friend Rita began a program to help little "Muni." As a result of fundraising and advocacy, Muni could eventually smile for the very first time in her life. Because of Rita's loving-kindness, the seed of compassion was watered in a worldwide community of friends who found ways to open their hearts to relieve suffering and offer a new life for this now-young woman in India.

Practices to Develop Compassion

1. **Never turn away.** As we learned in India, allow yourself to be open to the suffering of others. This is the first step that often motivates us to take compassionate action. In India, "Namaste!" was a common greeting that gave us a chance to stop and see the oneness that existed between us and the untouchable children. This reminder still allows me to keep my eyes and heart open when connecting with a homeless person.

2. **Practice mindful breathing.** One of the best ways to be there for another person is to return to your breath. To be present with others and ourselves we can simply recite, "Breathing in, I am aware of this present moment. Breathing out, I embrace this moment."

3. **Listen deeply.** Reassure another by your presence. By listening deeply, you can let them know that they are the most important person in that moment and that, regardless of what is said, you will not turn away. Deep listening is a powerful way to relieve suffering.

4. **Look deeply.** Focus on what is being touched in you as you interact with another and try not to turn away from the pain that is emerging. Often someone's pain will touch something deep in your consciousness, which is often connected to some kind of unfinished business from your own past. Use this an opportunity to learn more about yourself.

Joy

If you are having a wonderful day, most likely you have nurtured joy in yourself or connected with a joyful person. Thich Nhat Hanh's classic book, *Teachings on Love* defines joy as a feeling of peace and contentment. "We rejoice when we see others happy, but we rejoice in our own well-being as well. How can we feel joy for another person when we do not feel joy for ourselves? Joy is for everyone." He also writes, "True love always brings joy to ourselves and the one we love. If it does not bring joy, it is not true love."

Think of people in your life who personify joy in their daily work. It could be a server in your favorite restaurant or the person who smiles at you on the subway. People often reflect on the qualities the Dalai Lama personifies—his smile and overall feeling of joy. Everyone feels better when they are around him, as he notices others and truly connects on a deep personal level.

Practices to Develop Joy

1. **Say "Yes."** Experience what is here and now. Be open to the pleasant and the unpleasant. When we say "no" we stop our breath, and when we say "yes" it allows the breath to be open fully to life.

2. **Linger longer.** Look around and see what is beautiful in your life. It takes only 10 breaths to rewire your brain in positive ways. When we register an event and store it in our consciousness, that helps sustain the feeling in the future.

3. **Practice gratitude.** One of the best avenues to joy is gratitude. Look around and be grateful for what you have and avoid worrying about what you think you need in order to be happy. What are the conditions and people that you are grateful for? Health, family, friends, livelihood, food and shelter? Those moments in which you allow gratitude to truly sink into your consciousness are moments that carry with them great joy.

Equanimity

Equanimity is the groundwork for love. Without the stability of equanimity, we are unable to truly understand another (loving-kindness), to be there when they are suffering (compassion), and to bring our loving spirit to share with another (joy). The word "equanimity" has Latin roots in "even" and "mind." Our ancient circuitry of the brain is continually driving us to be one way or another—restful or reactive. When I am out of balance, I am aware that equanimity is like a barometer and a reminder to bring myself back to a more even-minded place—not too high or not too low.

Practices to Develop Equanimity

1. **Take refuge.** We all need a personal inner space of peace and safety, like birds seeking refuge, returning to a familiar place time and again. With mindfulness as our practice, our first place of refuge is to return to the present.

2. **Transform habit energy.** Our tendency is to react automatically when confronted with challenging people and stressful situations. Over a lifetime, we have typically learned to

condition and armor ourselves with an automatic response rather than taking on the stance of witness. Our response may often add to the angst of the moment and create more hostility. Are you aware of your response to indifference, harsh words or anger in others?

3. **Let go of attachments.** One of my favorite sayings is "Attachments are the root of all suffering." Typical attachments include our identity with our body image, specific people, our career, material goods, thoughts, feelings and anything that causes us to create a fixed view of how things are and should be. If I am attached to how I want another person to be, I will suffer, and so will they. If I am attached to how I wish something to turn out, I will suffer if it does not turn out the way I want. If I am attached to being right, I will suffer rather than be happy.

Contemplations

For all of us, love can be the natural state of our own being; naturally at peace, naturally connected, because this becomes the reflection of who we simply are.

—SHARON SALZBERG

In the face of suffering, one has no right to turn away, not to see.

—ELIE WIESEL

Works of love are always works of joy.

—MOTHER TERESA

Equanimity means nonattachment, nondiscrimination, even-mindedness, or letting go. You climb the mountain to be able to look over the whole situation, not bound by one side or the other.

—THICH NHAT HANH

Questions to Ponder

- What are the traits you find in individuals you like to be with? Create your own list and discover for yourself how mindfulness is often one of the key qualities we value most in others.

- Think about the most important people in your life. Consider how you might apply this strategy of mindfulness to your next interaction with them? How might you practice the qualities of loving-kindness, compassion, joy and equanimity? What are the typical distractions that prevent you from being truly present for another individual? Use each person as a reminder to be mindful. How can you create more mindful moments with those you love?

PART FIVE
Deepening

People will do anything, no matter how absurd, in order to avoid facing their own souls. One does not become enlightened by imagining figures of light, but by making the darkness conscious. —**CARL JUNG**

IN PART FIVE YOU WILL

- Explore a process of looking deeply
- Discover how unfinished business keeps us from living in the present
- Explore a pathway to becoming a part-time mystic

Looking Deeply

When your mindfulness becomes powerful, your concentration becomes powerful, and when you are fully concentrated, you have a chance to make a breakthrough, to achieve insight.

—THICH NHAT HANH

Now we have a chance to expand on and use what we are learning, while we look deeply at ourselves. In all forms of meditation there are three components—mindfulness, concentration and insight. When I first started to meditate, I thought that mindfulness and concentration were enough to manage the stress of life. They were an important foundation and helped me to feel less anxious and more present. Yet this was not enough to create a transformation of the behaviors that led me to a stressful place. I found myself wanting more; looking deeply was the needed piece to create insight.

At a retreat led by Thich Nhat Hanh, when drinking a cup of tea, I was reminded to stop and calm myself to totally enjoy the fragrance and flavor of the tea. When my mind became distracted, it was difficult to savor each sip. Yet with a breath, I was able to return to the tea. With mindfulness and concentration, I experienced the tea fully, and by continuing to look deeply it was possible to see the sun that warmed the tea leaves, the rain that watered the plants, and the workers harvesting the tea in the fields.

My cup of tea was more than tea; it encompassed everything.

In this final section, we will explore ways to deepen our practice of mindfulness, starting with learning to use our breath as an anchor for being in the moment and as a guide to exploring our body, feelings, perceptions, mental formations and consciousness.

Breathing!

Breathing is the foundation of mindfulness. It is the quality that makes the present moment more alive. It is also a guide for shining light on what is arising in our awareness and helping us gain insight and understanding. We looked at how to practice mindful breathing earlier in this book. Now I invite you to go a little deeper.

Mindful Breathing Practice

1. Find a comfortable sitting position, with your back straight. Relax your hands and arms, or place them in your lap. Once you have learned this exercise, you may choose to keep your eyes either open or closed.
2. Bring your awareness to your breath. Do not change your breathing, but simply observe and experience the in and out movement of air through your nose or the rising and falling of your diaphragm. Connect the in-breath to the out-breath, the out-breath to the in-breath.
3. Now as you read the following prompts, allow yourself to go deeper and experiment with your breath.

- What is like to settle in and just observe your breath as it is? One or two breaths may help to restore yourself.

- What is like when you take a deep breath, following the breath from your nostrils, all the way down, allowing your abdomen to rise? Follow that breath all the way back out of your body.

- While breathing slowly, are you aware of the spaces between the in-breath and out-breath? When we notice the space in our breath and in our life, that awareness allows us to connect to with a silent mystery that is deeper and beyond ourselves—God, the Ultimate, the Divine or nature.

- Now be aware of taking a slow breath. Become aware that at any time you can adjust your breathing to adjust to the situation. If you are feeling stress, replace that emotion by taking a few slow deep breaths.

- Now become aware of your breath. Breathing in, smile and recognize that this moment is a wonderful moment. Notice how quickly, with a smile, you are able to change your mood.

- When confronted with any issue, use the breath as a chance to settle into your body.

Mindful breathing can offer us physical and mental equilibrium, as it is the mediator between our mind and body. Together, we will shine light on what are called the five aggregates—a Buddhist term—that make up the qualities found in the present moment. In exploring these qualities, we will discover the foundation of our physical, emotional and spiritual well-being.

Looking Deeply at What Arises

Take a moment to reflect on your breath. Recognize that when you are focused on one thing, such as breathing, you automatically become more relaxed. Notice how easy your focus will habitually take you away from your breath—as sensations in your body arise, feelings surface, thoughts and our perceptions take over and mental formations or stories hijack your awareness.

Body

Recently I had the unnerving experience of waking up with a back spasm so severe it took enormous energy to even attempt to get out of bed. In that moment, I was highly attuned to the messages of my body—severely constricted back muscles, painful tension in my entire body, constricted breathing, and subsequent fear and panic.

It was easier for me to minimize the impact of this pain by breathing and becoming aware of what was happening. I quickly understood that my body initiated a stress response exacerbated by my feelings of fear. By stopping and calming myself in that moment, the wrenching pain gradually subsided and I could eventually get up and get help.

The best doorway to the present moment and barometer to gauge our well-being is to check in with our body. One of my favorite quotes from Rumi is, "Do you pay regular visits to yourself?"

- What are you seeing, hearing, tasting, smelling and touching?

- How are you breathing? From your chest? Your diaphragm? Is your breathing labored?

- What are your heart rate and muscle tension telling you about what's happening now?

- Are there places in your body that bring up old memories from both physical and emotional scars?

- Where and what is stored in your body, causing ongoing suffering?

Learning mindfulness begins with learning to check in with our bodies. As Alice Miller said, "The truth about our childhood is stored up in our body. And although we can repress it, we can never alter it. Our intellect can be deceived, our feelings manipulated, our perceptions confused, and our body tricked with medication. But someday the body will present its bill."

Feelings

We record memories of our lives in terms of the positive and negative experiences that influence our overall mood and offer depth to each moment. When we recall significant experiences in our lives, we can rediscover moments in which our current thoughts and feelings were first activated. In working with groups, I often ask, "When did you feel most alive? Describe that moment." People often share tender or powerful moments such as the birth of a child, experiencing a brilliant sunset, or the antics of a playful puppy. What memories activate feelings that cause you to wonder about your worth? What memories create feelings of sadness, anger, anxiety or doubt even years later?

In elementary school, I always seemed to be getting into some kind of trouble with my teachers. It's probably safe to say that, given the advances in medicine and psychology over the years, I would most likely have been diagnosed with what is now known as ADHD (attention deficit hyperactivity disorder). Without access to today's knowledge of this disorder, my teachers were naturally confused about how best to support my learning experiences. Often my hyperactivity was seen as a behavioral issue, and I was disciplined accordingly, including once being locked in the janitor's closet during a school movie. In the fourth grade, I spent a whole year in what was called "the rotten apple row"—designated for students the teacher labeled "troublemakers." As we know, one rotten apple spoils the whole barrel.

This embarrassment and shame caused me to doubt myself and created the feeling of not being enough. During my life, I found myself working harder to prove myself, to show the world that I was somebody; these were clearly ego-based responses. As I reflect back on my life, I suspect one of the reasons I became a professor of education was to help to rectify conditions in the schools so to make sure other children didn't have such a bad experience.

Feelings are typically pleasant, unpleasant or neutral. Every day these feelings wake us up or lull us into a state of complacency. Learning to look deeply and discover the source of these feelings is the essence of mindfulness.

Perceptions

Our thoughts are so powerful, they can quickly turn into ideas or judgments about our self and others. By stopping, calming, and looking deeply, we can recognize when these perceptions are not accurate. One of my favorite practices is to ask, "Am I sure?"

Can you recall a situation in which you created a view about something or someone that turned out to be totally false? Such perceptions begin with thoughts that then become distorted. I recall receiving a beautiful needlepoint as a gift from my sister-in-law following a family vacation on the coast. We placed it prominently in our home as a constant reminder of our wonderful time together. Several months later, we mentioned how many beautiful memories were evoked by the needlepoint. She asked, "Did you notice the blemish in the corner?" So often our mind overlooks the overall beauty and goes directly to the tiny flaw, which is rarely noticed.

Perceptions often become deceptions because of our natural tendency to get caught on the negative while positive perceptions disappear like the proverbial water off a duck's back. With mindfulness as my guide, I am able to step back and witness the rational or irrational nature of my ongoing perceptions. This practice helps me gain a clear understanding of what is taking place in this moment. It reminds me of standing, as I did recently, by the side of an ocean inlet on a still evening. The mountains behind me were beautifully mirrored in the water's surface, reflecting what is true and what is real.

Mental Formations: The Stories of Our Lives

As we explore the qualities of the present moment, we realize that our perceptions are formed over time. Gardens are physical formations that have been nurtured over the years and shaped by infinite conditions—the sun, the moon, rain, soil, compost and numerous seeds. Similarly, we begin with a sperm and an egg, which creates a zygote; then we become an embryo in our mother's womb, and after birth, our physical self grows from an infant to an adult. Our bodies are shaped by countless conditions from the time of our birth. So, too, our ever-changing feelings are molded by our experiences and interactions until they become strong mental formations.

A friend recently shared the challenges he had with his father during childhood. His father became easily angered, and my friend wondered if he had that same potential for anger. Our discussion turned to mindfulness, and by looking deeply he began to see that the seeds of his father's anger were also in him. He recalled becoming easily angered by insignificant events, and how similar his actions were to his father's. The father's anger watered the same seeds in the son, allowing them to grow deep and, under certain conditions, to erupt many years later.

Mental formations are the stories we create from our experiences. Perhaps they start with a physical pain, which leads to feelings and perceptions of anxiety or fear. We replay these stories in the middle of the night when we are unable to sleep; each is like a piece of music that plays repeatedly in our minds.

Mental formations are stored in the soil of our consciousness as seeds. Seeds are made up from our thoughts, feelings and perceptions. When these seeds are triggered by an experience or event, they spring up in the mind consciousness as a mental formation. For example, in the soil of my consciousness, the seed of fear lies dormant alongside many other seeds, such as awareness and faith.

When I experience an event that is fear-based, like the covid-19 scare, it will trigger other similar memories and stories from my life that were fear-based. It may ignite memories about when I was young and my parents were worried about a family member who was seriously ill, or about the death of my grandparents. Using mindfulness, I am able to recognize that the fear in the moment is also related to all my previous experiences of fear. We see the connections, which helps us understand ourselves and our mental formations with more clarity.

Consciousness

The final pathway leading us deeply into the present moment is consciousness, which includes the mind consciousness—what is happening in the present, and the store consciousness—what has happened in the past. A metaphor I like to use is that the mind consciousness represents the visible garden, and the soil and seeds represent the store consciousness. Every experience in our lives has influenced the seeds in our consciousness. Every time we water or give attention to one seed or another, we create a story or mental formation, and that seed becomes active in our mind consciousness. The longer we keep the seed alive in our mind, the stronger its roots become in our soil consciousness.

For example, the longer I am angry with someone, the more likely I am to remain angry and to become angry more often. This explains why a person may erupt violently after a minor situation; the current anger is a manifestation of all the anger that was experienced and stored in the past. Just as a garden needs a variety of elements to grow, so does a beautiful, vibrant life. It's important to pay attention to the process of how we cultivate our store consciousness, which includes soil, seeds and compost.

Having developed our practice of mindfulness, we can more easily observe the seeds that lie deep within our consciousness and learn how to water or transform these qualities. We learn how to aerate the soil so there is healthy circulation between the soil and the garden of our consciousness—the store and mind consciousness. Healthy circulation means that you allow both the positive and negative qualities to emerge into your awareness. Soon you will discover how the quality of your life depends on which seeds you have watered, and which seeds you have allowed others to nurture throughout your life.

As I will discuss later, consciousness also includes our connection with all beings. Carl Jung, called this the "collective unconscious." Through this exploration, we'll discover that although we may sometimes think we are alone, we are always connected by irrefutable and deep-seated beliefs, including our spirituality and life and death instincts. Jung suggests that due to our ancestral heritage, every person is born with thoughts and images that we share with others. This aspect of our deeper selves cannot be changed by mindfulness, yet the practice of mindfulness allows us to become aware of these ineffable qualities.

Contemplations

Looking deeply at life as it is in this very moment,
the meditator dwells in stability and freedom.

—THE BUDDHA

Looking deeply, we see that only wisdom and
compassion can solve delusions.

—ROSHI JOAN HALIFAX

Nothing ever goes away until it teaches us
what we need to know.

—PEMA CHODRON

Questions to Ponder

First Practice

Find a comfortable place that allows for complete relaxation with no interruptions, and create an opportunity to become aware of your immediate environment, including the following:

- What am I seeing? What colors and shapes? What beauty?
- What am I hearing? Birds, people, cars?
- What is happening in my body at this moment? What type of breathing am I experiencing? Do I feel pain or tension in my muscles, or a state of relaxation?
- What feelings are the most challenging to be with?
- As I reflect on my feelings about a person or interpret a situation I am struggling with, I can ask myself, "Am I sure?"
- What stories continue to play in my mind? Can I unearth the origin of this story or mental formation?
- What positive qualities or seeds were watered in my life that brought me to this place and time?

Second Practice

Take a moment to find a comfortable position and become aware of your breathing. As you do so, say to yourself:

Breathing in, I am aware that I am breathing in.
Breathing out, I am aware that I am breathing out.
Breathing in, I hear the sound of the birds.
Breathing out, I smile.
Breathing in, I am aware of tension in my body.
Breathing out, I release my tension.
Breathing in, I am aware of the preciousness of this day.
Breathing out, I vow to live deeply in this day.

Unfinished Business

What you choose not to look at in your life rules your life.

—LYNN ANDREWS

In the process of quieting your mind and becoming more mindful, you will most likely become aware of what is unfinished in your life. Your efforts to live mindfully may be hampered by this unfinished business, which the late death and dying specialist Dr. Elisabeth Kübler-Ross defines as "something that is incomplete in our lives that deprives us of a sense of peace." Most unfinished business involves relationships and can include the most challenging and traumatic events that have happened in our lives.

How often do you reflect on things you wish you had said to others? You might be asking yourself: Why didn't I say, "I love you"? Why didn't I thank him? You might wish you had made peace with your dad before he died, or your child, or a friend.

Unfinished business can serve as a reminder to say the "I love you" *now*. Send those flowers to a loved one *now*. Appreciate someone *now*. Forgive someone *now*. Completing your unfinished business allows you to let go of the past and live more fully in the present moment. As you examine your life, goals and relationships, ask yourself, "What is unfinished? What baggage from the past do I carry with me today? What robs me of a sense of peace?"

Unfinished business can be about those who are alive and those who are deceased. Examples include "Why didn't we take that trip to Hawaii we dreamed about *before* she developed terminal cancer?" It includes things we have said or not said. Often, regrets trickle out as resentments toward others and can be the core of challenging relationships. Unfinished business is often about unresolved grief. It can be a residue of rejections, broken promises and abandonments, or it can be linked to unfulfilled dreams, betrayals and a loss of faith. Unresolved issues may also be at the core of a serious life trauma.

You don't need to carry the burden of unfinished business throughout your lifetime. There are some meaningful techniques for getting closure or healing old wounds. For example:

Letter Writing

- You may choose to write a letter to a loved one expressing your appreciation, as well as your hurt or resentments. However, the important part is that you DO NOT SEND such a letter if you have filled it with anger and accusations, or you may create more unfinished business for yourself. The key is to release the negative feelings in a healthy way.

- This can also be a healthy grieving process if you did not share your true feelings with someone who has died. Write a letter to this individual and pour out your heart, hopefully releasing your unfinished business. Then, and only when you feel ready, write a letter back to yourself from the person who died! It may sound strange, but it can be a very healing experience. You will unknowingly begin to tap into the true heart of the loved one and "hear" what you needed to hear when they were alive.

Rituals

- Rituals can be a healing way to let go! You could plant a tree, or flower, or whatever reminds you of your connection with the person. My wife Kathleen, a grief counselor, is a proponent of rituals. On several occasions, we planted trees to remember a loved one, including one of our pets. Another ritual could involve going to the ocean or lake to release a loved one's cremains with good wishes or a prayer. Individuals, as well as families, can create memory books or a scholarship to remember with peace rather than anger or resentment.

Trauma and Unfinished Business

Psychologically speaking, all experiences stay with us until we achieve closure. Some of these events may never be completely resolved because of the severity of the trauma involved.

According to the American Psychological Association, "Trauma is an emotional response to a terrible event like an accident, rape or natural disaster. Immediately after the event, shock and denial are typical. Longer-term reactions include unpredictable emotions, flashbacks, strained relationships and even physical symptoms like headaches or nausea. While these feelings are normal, some people may have difficulty moving on with their lives."

Sometimes the core of unfinished business is related to early pain, abuse and trauma. If these are a recurring story for you and your life is continually affected by these experiences, consider seeking professional assistance. Mindfulness-based methods, including Mindfulness-Based Stress Reduction (MBSR), Mindfulness-Based Cognitive Therapy (MBCT), and Metta—

loving kindness meditations—are often helpful. The longer we linger on these stories, the more likelihood there is for re-traumatization.

Bessel van der Kolk, a pioneering trauma researcher, said, "The past is alive in the form of gnawing interior discomfort. Their bodies are constantly bombarded by visceral warning signs, and in an attempt to control these processes they often become expert at ignoring their gut feelings and in numbing awareness of what is played out inside. They learn to hide from their selves." The short title of his book, *The Body Keeps the Score*, offers an understanding of how trauma not only lives in our consciousness, it is also alive in our body.

Elaine Miller-Karas, author of *Building Resilience to Trauma*, describes trauma as an individual's perception of an event as threatening to oneself or others. Traumatic memories from the past, triggered in the present moment, take us back in time and hold us captive there. It is as if we are living that past moment right here and now. The senses in our body, our feelings and emotions, our thoughts, and even what we consider to be reality have been hijacked. The experience may have happened last week, last month or last year, or even during our childhood. These memories, once they are triggered, can take our stable, clear-thinking mind offline, and we become trapped in the past. But neuroscience has taught us ways to quiet the alarmed brain and allow our present-moment brain to come back online.

How to Work with Unresolved Trauma

- **Be aware that your natural bias is toward negativity.** The fight/flight/freeze responses in our ancient minds allowed humans to survive. Recalling Schneider's *Ten Breaths to Happiness, this* practice is a helpful aid to counter our negativity bias and strengthening our neural pathways toward happiness, connection and well-being.

Elaine Miller-Karas says these kinds of practices can expand our personal resources, building "internal resiliency and a renewed sense of one's own abilities and capacity to stabilize the nervous system." These experiences then become resources—powerful experiential memories we can call on in times of difficulty to bring us back into the present moment, where we can see that we really are okay right now.

- **Ground yourself to the Earth.** We are held on this Earth by gravity. When we are taken away to the past, we can feel ungrounded, or maybe overly grounded. Touching the Earth, feeling the pull of the Earth holding us on this planet, is a great way to keep us in the present moment. One of Thich Nhat Hanh's favorite practices is walking meditation. During the difficult times of war in Vietnam, he practiced slow, mindful walking meditation outside or even in his small room. In walking meditation, we bring our attention to our feet on the ground; all our energy is invested there. We notice the movement of each step as we lift, roll, and place our foot back on the ground. But grounding can be done in many ways. As we work at our desk, we can feel the solidity of our feet on the floor. This simple practice can keep us anchored in the present moment.

- **Notice and slow down gestures.** Take three seconds to think about a self-soothing gesture, such as placing your hand on your heart. Or think about a gesture of confidence, such as a thumbs up, or a gesture of joy, such as a verbal "Yay!" Count slowly to three and then make this gesture. As you make this gesture, notice what happens inside. Allow that internal experience to unfold and deepen. A "butterfly hug" is a movement used by a friend who offers workshops around the world for people who have been traumatized by war. It is a simple action of crossing your hands over your chest and alternately clapping each shoulder softly. It is a soothing response and a way to love yourself.

- **Pay attention to sensations and take gentle care of your activated mind.** Bring your attention to your body and notice what sensations are present—pleasant, unpleasant or neutral. When sensations in your body are pleasant or neutral, it is easy to be in the present moment. But what about agitation, the shock of fear, the dagger of hurt, or any of a myriad of difficult physical sensations you may be experiencing? Whether it is remembering a trauma or just responding to something upsetting in the present moment, you can take gentle care of your mind and body.

When negative or unwanted emotions and sensations are activated, we have a choice. We can allow ourselves to be carried away by what we are experiencing—or we can stop. Even if it's only for a fleeting moment, we can gently shift our attention to powerful positive memories or to our sense of groundedness with the Earth, feeling the experience with our whole body. Or we can practice gesturing. Thus, we shift our attention away from a distressing experience and take refuge in wholesome, positive, nurturing experiences of our body and mind. We build our strength and capacity to weather the storms we all encounter and to more fully live an authentic life of stability and happiness in the present moment.

A traditional Zen story illustrates the importance of shifting our awareness in order to find well-being. In the story, two monks were walking along a road and came to a river. On the bank was a beautiful young woman who was afraid to cross the river by herself. One of the monks gallantly stepped forth and offered her a ride on his shoulders. Upon reaching the other side, she thanked the monk and they went their separate ways. After they had resumed their walk down the road, the second monk asked the first, in agitation, "How could you do that? You are a monk, a renunciate! You should not be carrying beautiful women around on your shoulders." To which the first monk replied, "Oh, are you still carrying her? I let her down when we reached the shore."

Contemplations

What is left ungrieved remains stored in our body,
heart and soul. It can come out each time
we experience loss anew.

—ELISABETH KUBLER-ROSS

The remedy is not to suppress negative experiences;
when they happen, they happen. Rather, it is to foster
positive experiences—and in particular, to take them in
so they become a permanent part of you.

—RICK HANSON

Questions to Ponder

Take some time to ponder the following questions, which offer a key to how you are living your life.

- Are you preoccupied with the thought of a negative encounter with someone?
- Do you cry easily or get angry at the thought of this person or experience?
- Do you have a history of trauma that influences your health today?
- Are you caught in a story about your past that continues to be a focus of your awareness?
- Are your thoughts frequently prefaced by "If only …"?
- Do you find yourself becoming emotionally involved with another person's problems whose troubles are similar to your own?
- What are you currently putting off in your life?
- If you are unable to resolve a conflict or complete unfinished business with another person, is it possible to make peace with the situation? Can you accept the reality that things are broken and may never be resolved?

- Are there experiences or traumas in your life that may simply require more time and space before you can attempt to heal them?

- After reflecting on the traditional Zen story earlier in the chapter: What are you still holding onto in your life?

The Part-Time Mystic

Your True Self is Life and Being and Love. Love is what you were made for and love is who you are.

—**RICHARD ROHR**

Mindfulness has been a life changer for me! With the practice, I began to feel more relaxed and less anxious. Almost immediately I felt a release of my stress. But I soon realized there was something even deeper going on, something that was naturally facilitated by stopping, pausing, breathing and calming. Mindfulness opened the door to an understanding of the mystical path.

With this practice as a foundation, I started to look more deeply. I wondered: What would it be like to be a "part-time mystic"? The word "mystic" invoked mystery, an enticing invitation. I explored the derivation of the word and found that it pertains to mysteries of faith. From the 14th-century Old French language comes mistique, which means "mysterious, full of mystery." Latin has given us mysticus, which means "mystical, mystic, of secret rites."

I began to create time for spiritual reading and contemplation and found myself drawn to a local Trappist Monastery. The monks live in a cloistered setting and they organize their life around prayer, study, work and hospitality. They are modern-day mystics who live simply and devote their days to seeking connection with all, especially God. They are seeking their "True self"— their absolute identity, soul or greater self. Some people would call this our "God Self" or the "branch connected to the vine" (John 15:5). Others would call it our Buddha nature, or higher self.

Ultimately, it's all about connections. At the Trappist Abbey, I feel as if I can touch the Ultimate dimension when looking at a flower with the eyes of Interbeing. I see the sun that warms the flower, the rain that moistens its leaves and roots, the compost the flower will become. Everything, I am learning, is one. When we are aware of these greater connections, our thoughts naturally turn toward God, the Divine, the Ultimate, nature or whatever we choose to call this ineffable force. The Ultimate has a different meaning for each of us. Evelyn Underhill, an Anglican Catholic writer and mystic, gave us the classical definition of mysticism. She wrote that "mysticism in its pure form, is the science of Ultimates, the science of union with the Absolute, and nothing else, and the mystic is the person who attains to this union."

Walk with me as I share the path of the mystic. Although I am still a beginner, this path has begun to answer some of my deepest desires. It may do the same for you.

Reflections on the Path of the Mystic

Famous mystics included John of the Cross, Teresa of Avila, Julian of Norwich, the Sufi Rumi, Ravi Shankar, Meister Eckhart and Thomas Merton. But there are many everyday people who aspire to this type of union. They could be called part-time mystics or, as Tom Stella coined the term, "mediocre mystics." The Latin root of *mediocre* is mediocris, which means "halfway up a mountain." We may not attain the spiritual heights we aspire to and that others have reached, but we all have that potential.

Stella, a spiritual teacher and a lifelong student of the Catholic mystic, Thomas Merton, defines two qualities found in the mystic. First, they are able to open themselves to their "shadow," and second, they are "lovers."

Darkness to Light

When we slow down, stop, and allow ourselves to be alone, we often come in touch with who we really are. We touch all the parts of ourselves, including the things we tend to bury and avoid because they create too much pain and suffering. Often, we spend most of our lives being busy, while unconsciously avoiding another side of ourselves. Jon Kabat-Zinn titled one of his books *Full Catastrophe Living*. The title is borrowed from the 1964 film, "Zorba the Greek," which follows a colorful man with a zest for life. Zorba tells his boss that he has a "wife, children, house—everything. The full catastrophe." For Kabat-Zinn, the phrase embodies the richness of life with its full complement of dilemmas, sorrows, tragedies and ironies. In my own life, I know that without suffering, there can be no happiness. The lotus flower won't bloom without the mud.

The phrase "dark night of the soul" came from the writings of a 16th-century mystic, John of the Cross. His work inspired other mystics and authors, and especially inspired Carl Jung, a Swiss psychiatrist who popularized the concept. Jung spoke about our "shadow," the part of our personality consigned to the darkness of our unconscious. According to author Eckhart Tolle, "the dark night of the soul can be brought on by an external event, such as a natural disaster, a life-changing medical diagnosis, or the death of a loved one." As I write this chapter, our world is facing the coronavirus pandemic, which is causing many of us to question everything and feel like our society has hit bottom. Never have the consequences been so grave for so many, and for some people, life's meaning has disintegrated. This is truly a global dark night of the soul. In more personal terms, the dark night of the soul sometimes appears about 3 o'clock in the morning, when we lie awake with worry and despair.

Psychologist Robert Masters suggests that our shadow "is the place within each of us that contains what we don't know, don't like, or deny about ourselves." Our work is to explore the deep crevices of our consciousness and acknowledge the parts of ourselves that we have denied. With that awareness, we can learn to accept all parts of ourselves—and others. We learn that our shadow does not need to control us and that we can find ways to let go and live more fully in the present. In so doing, we will be more open to loving ourselves and others.

Mystics Are Lovers

Along with the ability to befriend their inner darkness, the mystic is smitten; they are in love with God, people, life—with something or someone greater than themselves. At an international meeting of preachers, the group was discussing what it took to be a good preacher. Some said a good preacher spends long hours in prayer. Others said he or she would know the scriptures. Another said humor was the most important quality. At last, a woman from Africa said, "Good preachers are in love." It doesn't matter who or what they are in love with, but simply that they are in love. Passionate preaching comes out of a love affair with God, the Divine, the Absolute, and that love transfers to everyone they meet. The human dimension of love is essential to the mystical path. We are not separate, and we all have the same needs: love, acceptance and connection.

To follow this path and pursue these teachings, we need to

find kindred spirits who are interested in walking together. In the Celtic world, *anam* means soul, and *cara* is the word for friend. We can call these kindred spirits *anam cara*—soul friends. They are able to accept us despite our woundedness. They can shine the light that creates understanding. Often, we are not aware of our own challenges and shadows. With these kinds of relationships, we are able to grow. This growth is sometimes dependent on honest reflections from those who accept us unconditionally.

Having a partner or good friend—or friends—is essential to our ongoing development. We can't do this work alone. Stephen Cope, who wrote *Soul Friends: The Transforming Power of Deep Human Connection*, said, "A soul friend can be a person we are or were in relationships with or it can be an historical figure we never met." This friend offers us a mirror for our growth; they challenge us. They also recognize our creativity, vulnerability and potential, and see us as unique.

For me, it has always been important to have several soul friends—or anam caras—with whom I can share my innermost mind and heart. My wife of more than 35 years has been a constant wellspring, offering insights and support along the way. I have also relied on teachers such as Carl Rogers, Ram Dass and Thich Nhat Hanh. By their presence and through their writings, these luminaries have offered a map for my journey. Several close friends illuminate these teachings and are not afraid to share what they see in me.

This union with something greater than ourselves is a developmental phenomenon and not often experienced until the second half of our lives. During the first part, we seek to become "Somebody," and our striving is typically connected to societal norms that worship success, status and ownership. Our eagerness for success is driven by our ego, and it sometimes seems as if we can never get enough to satisfy. This is not necessarily bad, as it is a passing hunger. Usually, we feel the strongest ego-striving during the first part of our lives, but sooner or later we discover that status and perennial grasping does not give us the love and happiness we seek. As Thomas Merton wrote, "We may spend our whole life climbing the ladder of success, only to find when we get to the top the ladder is leaning against the wrong wall."

We can begin to let go of the preoccupation with our egoic selves by being aware of how much we talk about ourselves, and the pronouns we use: I, me, mine. Parts of our ego must die before we can realize our true self. Recently, Charles Busch, a friend and former minister, recently offered a toast at his father's 85th birthday party. Charles said, "In all the years that I have known my father, I never heard him say a word of praise for himself. Not once. Nothing to make himself shine in the eyes of others. On the other hand, in all those years, I never heard him say a negative word about himself. Not even 'That was stupid of me.'" Charles wasn't sure what to call this trait. Finally, when he read the words from Gandhi, it came to him: "No word or pose in self-promotion, no word or gesture of self-depreciation." Charles came up with the word "zero." Perhaps that is why his father never commented to him about his toast.

True love is one of the most important guideposts on our journey, for the part-time mystic's greatest aspiration is to be a lover of all and to find union with their God, the Ultimate, their higher power, or the natural world. They are aware of our oneness and feel a sense of Interbeing.

A New Kind of Hope

Mystics have the courage and ability to befriend their inner darkness, but they also understand the importance of hope. Hope comforts us during times of adversity, uncertainty and fear. During difficult times, especially in the era of the coronavirus pandemic, we all need something to hold onto that is greater than ourselves. Franciscan Sister Ilia Delio reminds us that the typical kind of hope is based on the optimism that things will get better in the future. She offers a deeper way of cultivating hope, which she calls mystical, and which is not tied to a positive outcome in the future. Sister Delio says, "It lives a life of its own, seemingly without reference to external circumstances and conditions. It has something to do with *presence*—not a future good outcome, but the immediate experience of being met, held in communion, by something intimately at hand." This comes back to the practice of being aware and alive to what is happening in the present moment. Hope is a feeling that offers strength, joy and peace, a feeling not based on the desperate wish that outward circumstances will change. Rather, true hope is based on an inward understanding that sometimes we must simply accept the full catastrophe of life as it is.

Contemplations

Let nothing disturb you. Let nothing frighten you.
Everything passes away except God.

—ST. TERESA OF AVILA

You are understood as you are without mask or
pretension. The superficial and functional lies
and half-truths of social acquaintance fall away,
you can be as you really are.

—JOHN O'DONOHUE

Questions to Ponder

- What actions will you be remembered for? What will never die?
- How would you describe your "dark nights of the soul?" What keeps you awake at 3 a.m.?
- Mystics are lovers of all. What would that look like for you?
- In what ways do you sense a connection with the mystical dimension all that is beyond yourself?
- In today's world, a time of fear and anxiety—what gives you hope?

What's It All About?

Life can be found only in the present moment.
The past is gone, the future is not yet here, and if we do
not go back to ourselves in the present moment,
we cannot be in touch with life.

—THICH NHAT HANH

On a recent trip to Hawaii, I met a playwright who had written numerous Broadway and Hollywood productions. While having coffee together, I asked him if he had any secrets to share about writing. He replied, "People go to a play, or movie, or read books with the hope of getting at least one thought or inspiration. People typically will ask their friends, 'What was it all about?" In his writing, he hopes to leave his readers with at least one message that will add to their lives. In reflecting on the many messages offered in this book, I share with you some gems that can serve as simple reminders on how to incorporate this practice into your life.

Practicing Mindfulness: A Summary

- In our busy world, we frequently miss the opportunity to enjoy the little pleasures that are happening *now*. It is easy to forget that what brings us joy is often in front of us. When we practice mindfulness, we learn to stop and calm so we can truly see a child's smile, a beautiful sky, or a delicate spring flower.

- All forms of meditation and mindfulness training begin with a focus on the breath. Breathing can offer us physical and mental equilibrium as well as inner harmony.

- Most people breathe 17,000 to 24,000 times each day, yet few of us are aware of even one of those breathing cycles. Every passing moment our breath can create balance within us and bring us back to the present.

- By simply focusing on our inhaling and exhaling for ten breaths we can change the neural pathways in the brain. Instead of focusing on habitual patterns of anger and fear, we can focus on mindful breathing.

- With your awareness focused on the *in* and *out* of your breath, begin—without judgment and with patience—to explore your body, feelings and thoughts, and the stories you have created.

- When we meditate, there are many techniques for quieting the mind. Most techniques focus on a word, phrase, sound or object—such as the flame of a candle—to help us become more focused and centered.

- To cultivate a practice of returning to the present moment, consider ways in which you can stop, calm and look deeply at the phenomena of the present moment.

- Ancient cultures learned that naming our fears gives us a practical way to begin to gain power over them. Naming fears seems to demystify them and make them feel more benign.

- Accept negative feelings, such as fear, and then replace them with something more life-affirming. For example, in a loving-kindness meditation, we can replace fear or anger with love.

- When mindfulness is applied to eating, it becomes a powerful tool that can enhance the joy and beneficial effects of food.

- Overconsumption of negative news, combined with our own direct contact with pain and suffering, may produce cynical and depressing feelings. The more news we consume—especially when it creates fear and anger—the more likely it will rewire neuro pathways in our brain that are not conducive to well-being.

- The idea is to walk and enjoy the walking itself. That means learning to focus on the walking and not on the *destination*. Being is as important as *doing*.

- The qualities of loving-kindness, compassion, joy and equanimity are essential to healthy relationships. When we explore these qualities, we discover the best ways to create the understanding necessary to really love another.

- The best doorway to the present moment and barometer to gauge our well-being is to check in with our body.

- Feelings are typically pleasant, unpleasant or neutral. Every day these feelings wake us up or lull us into a state of complacency.

- We have a natural tendency to get caught on the negative, while positive perceptions can get lost. We can protect our happiness by intentionally focusing on the positive.

- Unfinished business almost always involves relationships and things that were said or left unsaid, done or not done. It also includes the most challenging and traumatic events that have happened in our lives.

- Mental formations are the stories we create from our experiences. They often wake us up in the middle of the night with feelings of anxiety and fear.

- When negative or unwanted emotions and sensations are activated, we have a choice. We can allow ourselves to be carried away by what we are experiencing—or we can stop. We can gently shift our attention from the past to a sense of groundedness with the Earth, and experience our whole body.

- Mindfulness is the beacon. When we stop, calm and look deeply, we become aware of our shadows and what is needed to love ourselves, others and the Divine. Mindfulness opens the door to an exploration of the mystical path.

- This level of awareness turns our thoughts toward God, the Divine, the Ultimate or nature.

- Mystics are open to themselves and their shadow. They are also lovers—in love with the Divine, people, nature, their lives. They feel passionate about the idea of something greater than themselves.

Thank you for walking this journey with me! Since I wrote the first edition of this book 25 years ago, the field of mindfulness—both research and practice—has grown dramatically and made significant inroads into society. In recent years, the concept and practice have only become more relevant. After a quarter-century of practicing mindfulness and meditation, I have come to believe there is no approach more effective for meeting the challenges of our era.

Together, we have looked at essential mindfulness practices. These practices offer peace and equanimity. They help people heal old wounds and find compassion for themselves and others. In the final section, we had an opportunity to go deeper, guided by the light of mindfulness. This deeper journey into a search for the Ultimate offers true transformation.

Mindfulness means to remember: We are only alive now, in this moment. The Dalai Lama said, "The past is past, and the future is yet to come. That means the future is in your hands—the future entirely depends on the present."

Moment by moment, breath by breath, we have the invitation and ability to create an abundant life. When we root ourselves in the present moment, we understand the preciousness of life. We become fully aware of each experience, we reawaken to beauty, and we discover a natural state of joy. The invitation is yours. Let the journey begin.

Mindfulness and Meditation Apps

These apps for smartphones and tablets (iOS and Android versions) are helpful for supporting one's daily mindfulness and meditation practice and connecting with worldwide practice communities. Enjoy!

The Insight Timer app supports your meditation with bells for daily practice and allows you to connect with a worldwide meditation community (https://insighttimer.com).

The Lotus Bud Mindfulness Bell offers a simple daytime reminder to mindfully awaken throughout your day (https://apps.apple.com/us/app/lotus-bud-mindfulness-bell/id502329366).

The Headspace app, featured in the *New York Times*, makes practicing simple mindfulness techniques easy (https://www.headspace.com/headspace-meditation-app).

The Mindfulness Bell app allows you to set a bell that rings randomly as a reminder to stop and breathe (https://apps.apple.com/us/app/mindfulness-bell/id380816407?mt=).

Bibliography

Bays, Chan Chozen. *Mindful Eating: A Guide to Rediscovering A Healthy and Joyful Relationship with Food*. Shambhala Publications, 2009.

Brach, Tara. *Radical Acceptance: Embracing Your Life with the Heart of a Buddha*. New York: Bantam, 2004.

Braza, Jerry. *Moment by Moment: The Art and Practice of Mindfulness*. Vermont: Tuttle Publishing, 1997

Braza, Jerry. *The Seeds of Love: Growing Mindful Relationships*. Vermont: Tuttle Publishing, 2011.

Busch, Charles. *Soft* as Water. Sweden: Irene Publishing, 2018.

Chodron, Pema. *When Things Fall Apart: Heart Advice for Difficult Times*. Shambhala, 2016.

Cope, Stephen. *Soul Friends: The Transforming Power of Deep Human Connection*. Hay House, 2017.

The Dalai Lama and Tutu, Desmond. *The Book of Joy: Lasting Happiness in a Changing World*. Avery, 2016.

Davis, Martha and Robbins, Elizabeth. *The Relaxation and Stress*

Reduction Workbook. New Harbinger, 2019.

Delio, Illio. *The Humility of God*. Franciscan Media, 2006.

Gach, Gary. *Pause Breathe Smile*. Boulder: Sounds True, 2018.

Goleman, Daniel and Davidson, Richard. *Altered Traits: Science Reveals How Mediation Changes your Mind, Brain and Body*. Avery, 2018.

Goldstein, Joseph. *Mindfulness: A Practical Guide to Awakening*. Sounds True, 2016.

Halifax, Joan. *Standing at the Edge*. New York: Flatiron Book, 2018.

Hanh, Thich Nhat. (Series): *How to Sit, How to Love, How to Walk, How to Eat*. Parallax Press, 2014-15.

———. *Miracle of Mindfulness*. Beacon Press, 1999.

———. *Living Buddha, Living Christ*. New York: Riverhead Books, 1995.

———. *Inside the Now*. Berkeley: Parallax Press, 2015.

———. *True Love*. Boston: Shambhala Publications, 2004

Hanson, Rick. *Hardwiring for Happiness*. New York: Harmony, 2013.

———. *The Practical Science of the Buddha's Brain*. Oakland:

New Harbinger, 2009

Kabat-Zinn, Jon. *Full Catastrophe Living*. Bantam, 2013.

Kahneman, Daniel. *Thinking Fast and Slow*. FSG, 2013.

Karas, Elaine Miller. *Building Resilience to Trauma and Community Resilience Models*. Routledge, 2015.

Kornfield, Jack. *A Path with Heart: A Guide Through the Perils and Promises of Spiritual Life*. New York, Bantam, 1993.

Linehan, Marsha. *Building a Life Worth Living*. Random House, 2020.

Masters, Robert. *Bringing Your Shadow Out of the Dark*. Sounds True, 2018.

Nghiem, Sister Dang. *Mindfulness as Medicine*. Berkeley: Parallax Press, 2015.

O'Donohue, John. *Anam Cara*. Harper Collins, 1998.

———. *To Bless the Space Between Us: A Book of Blessings*. Double Day, 2008.

Ostaseski, Frank. *The Five Invitations: Discovering What Death Can Teach Us About Living Fully*. Flatiron Books, 2019.

Radmacher, Mary Anne. *Lean forward into Your Life*. Conari Press, 2015.

Rohr, Richard. *Falling Upward: A Spirituality for the Two Halves of Life*. Jossey-Bass, 2011.

Salzberg, Sharon. *The Revolutionary Art of Happiness*. Shambhala Publications, 2002.

Schneider, Gary. *Ten Breaths to Happiness*. Berkeley: Parallax Press, 2009

Stella, Tom, *Finding God Beyond Religion*. Skylight Paths, 2013.

Suzuki, Shunryu, *Zen Mind, Beginner's Mind*, (50th Anniversary), Publications, 2020.

Teasdale, Wayne. *The Mystic Heart*. Novato: New World Library, 2001

Tolle, Eckhart. *The Power of Now*. Novato: The New World Library, 1999.

Van der Kolk, Bessel. *The Body Keeps the Score: Brain, Mind, and Body in the Healing of Trauma*. Penguin Books, 2015.

Williams, Florence. *The Nature Fix: Why Nature Makes Us Happier, Healthier, and More Creative*. New York: Norton, 2018

About the Author

For more than 35 years, Jerry Braza, Ph.D., has been a leading voice in the field of health, psychology and mindfulness. A professor emeritus from Western Oregon University, Jerry has worked with thousands of students and led hundreds of seminars, trainings, workshops and retreats focused on developing health and wellness through applied mindfulness practices. His experience includes work with hospitals, mental and behavioral health groups, and non-profit organizations.

Jerry's book, *Moment by Moment: The Art and Practice of Mindfulness*, was published in six languages and offers a beginner's guide to learning the practice. He also authored *The Seeds of Love: Growing Mindful Relationships*, which focuses on applying mindfulness to deepen the depth and quality of relationships.

You can catch Jerry's TED Talk about creating mindful communities at https://www.youtube.com/watch?v=o1poT8XW_qQ

For more information, visit www.theseedsoflove.net or contact Jerry at jfbraza@comcast.net.